LIFESKILLS WORKBOOK FOR ADULTS WITH AUTISM AND SPECIAL NEEDS

Activities to Help Develop Independence, Self-Advocacy, and Self-Care

Susan Jules

Get the Letter of Intent FOR FREE.

Sign up for the no-spam newsletter, and get the LETTER OF INTENT for free.

Details can be found at the end of the book.

The author and publisher have provided this e-book to you for your personal use only. You may not make this e-book publicly available in any way. Copyright infringement is against the law. If you believe the copy of this e-book you are reading infringes on the author's copyright, please notify us at diffnotless.com/piracy

TABLE OF CONTENTS

CHAPTER ONE

Introduction

a. Adults Living with Autism Spectrum Disorder and Other Special Needs

Autism is typically described as a neurological disorder that has a significant impact on one's learning and development. This implies that it is a condition that doesn't come about in adulthood. Rather, because of unawareness throughout history when it came to the appreciation, screening, and diagnosis of autism spectrum disorder (ASD), some people are diagnosed with ASD in adulthood; this is possible because of a missed diagnosis of the condition while the patients were younger.

Also, for individuals with ASD that were spotted in childhood, the condition does not vanish in adulthood. In particular cases, the correct kinds of interventions and provisions may help those individuals attain some level of independence and do things such as hold a job, be in meaningful relationships, and live on their own. However, these individuals may probably still contend with challenges because of having ASD, such as needing a quieter work environment to stay focused or maybe having puzzling instants in their relationships. Then in other cases, ongoing support and treatment aimed at meeting the individual's everyday needs would have to be sustained throughout adulthood, as autonomous living may not be probable.

For these and several other reasons, dealing with ASD and other forms of special needs in adults is a very tangible task, being one necessitating more means, and an improved understanding as explained by leading scientists in the field of autism study and advocacy. Recent studies in the last decade put forward that even though aftermaths for persons with ASD in some cases appeared to improve in adulthood, very pint-sized research has appraised adult functioning. This implies that even if individuals' childhood indications and impairments were to improve, scientists do not have an unblemished picture of where that leaves those individuals when it comes to living a characteristic adult life.

An additional part of the problem is that the means and support for persons with ASD gradually fade away once they enter adulthood. For instance, courtesy of legislation, comprising the Individuals with Disabilities Education Act (IDEA), children with the condition are qualified for access to treatment and educational services in the United States. However, a lot of those aids no longer apply to individuals once they turn twenty-one. Adults with ASD or other forms of special needs may be qualified to get medical and Social Security benefits to assist with basic needs like food and shelter, but then again resources for treatment and other services are more limited to older persons. The fact remains that most families do not always know how to get access to the services they need for their loved one as soon as they leave the school setting and venture into adulthood. This is one thing that a great number of researchers and clinicians agree upon unanimously.

Several critical issues that adults with ASD encounter may include transitioning out of a classroom environment, integrating into the workforce when the need arises, and circumventing discrimination.

b. Determining Next Steps

i. College, vocational school, or independent living. For individuals with ASD, life alterations come with unique trials and struggles, together with the shift from childhood to adulthood. But it is essential to keep in mind that everyone with ASD has varied experiences, not only in terms of their symptoms and what is most effective in managing their impairment but also in terms of how they can live in adulthood. Once they are done with school and they no longer have access to school counselors and the assembly of life in a classroom on which to rely, the transition is likely to be overwhelming.

Typically, if the person is leaving home to attend college, they leave behind their familiar social support of family and friends who know them, their symptoms, and needs too well. The moment they lose that day-to-day connection with their family and familiar environment, it can take a long time for them to establish such levels of connection with others.

However, a lot of people with ASD do go on to attend college or vocational schools learning specific trades, mainly those with high-functioning ASD, which was heretofore diagnosed as *Asperger's syndrome.* In some settings, colleges and universities have successfully made tailored programs and services developed to help meet the needs of people with ASD and other forms of special needs. Also in other settings, institutions have provided resources or made various forms of accommodations for people with ASD and other forms of special needs, some of which include the provision of notetakers or the allowance of students to wear items such as hats or tinted glasses to aid in the minimization of issues relating to sensory overload.

There are a lot of resources available that can help deepen one's understanding of how the Americans with Disabilities Act (ADA) applies to people with ASD or other forms of disability and special needs, and also how it can help with challenges such persons may encounter in a college setting. In addition, there are also several special programs, scholarships, and informational guides for people with autism that address these needs. Also, another act that could help determine the best next step in the transition from childhood into adulthood is having a chat with the school guidance counselor, school advisors, health-care providers, and other clinicians assisting in the management of the individual's condition.

ii. Holding jobs and entering the workforce. Regardless of where a person might fall on the autism spectrum, entering the workforce can spring up various hitches, comprising scuffles with employers and the ability to manage tasks that fall further than heretofore comfortable routines, and more. Nevertheless, the experience can be a real test for individuals with ASD or other forms of special needs, who must fine-tune to a work environment. Now, they would have to deal with coworkers and have to cordially get along with employers who might have little or no understanding of what it means to have ASD or a special need.

Regrettably, research has revealed that a good number of such encounters can lead to underemployment and even outright loss of employment for people with autism, even though these persons are intelligent enough to work. For instance, the unemployment rate for individuals who have disabilities in America as of February 2018 stood at 8.6 percent compared with 4.2 percent for people with no disabilities.

Furthermore, it can be extremely demanding for people with ASD and other forms of special needs, who might be fine with the physical demands of a job but who may find it almost impossible to interact socially with a customer. It is needless to state the level of feel and anxiety that they may feel in this kind of environment, as it could discourage them from seeking a job in the first place.

This is particularly demoralizing, as a lot of people with ASD or other forms of special needs do possess the intellectual capacity to hold a job, but not without the need for extra support in such a role compared to their contemporaries who do not have any form of the disorder. Now and again all they require is someone to coach them, to have patience, and offer support; but then again that can be hard to find.

A recent study which focused on the data of young individuals who received special education services over ten years, as well as 680 who had ASD, revealed that 34.7 percent of those young individuals with ASD attended college, with 55.1 percent of them able to hold down a job during the first six years after high school. Furthermore, the same study also showed that young individuals on the spectrum had the lowest rates of involvement in any kind of employment and the highest rates of zero participation after high school in comparison with people with other forms of special needs or disabilities.

c. The Rights of Adults with Autism Spectrum Disorder

The ADA legally safeguards people with ASD or any disability against any forms of discrimination that they might encounter in any fields or aspects of life ranging from employment and education to transportation and other public accommodations. This unique piece of legislation has many applications for people with ASD.

The ADA necessitates that an employer arranges for even-handed accommodations to an employee or a job applicant with any form of disability unless they would in some way jeopardize themselves or others by carrying out that role, and as long as they are otherwise competent for the role. The law also aids in ensuring that publicly funded housing openings are also accessible to people with ASD.

Persons with ASD may also be qualified to receive Medicaid benefits, depending on individual state programs and their enrolment criteria. Such services can help pay for long-term health-care expenses, as well as other elementary living necessities. Others may be qualified for Social Security benefits, too, which can also aid in covering the cost of elementary necessities. It must be noted that occasionally, prejudiced practices might not be obvious right away; this is why it is imperative for individuals with ASD or other forms of special needs to know their rights and recognize that a business cannot legally refuse services to anyone who might be displaying indications of being on the spectrum.

In addition, it is also critical to note that whether or not an individual makes known their ASD diagnosis to friends, family, or an employer is always their prerogative. In every situation, there are pros and cons to revealing sensitive information about one's disorder or disability. In the workplace, for instance, a revelation of such magnitude might lead to stigmatization, but then again, not revealing a disability might hinder one's employer from being legally obligated to make available special accommodations for potential needs. However, one's employer or human resource contact is obligated to keep such an admission confidential unless the employee wishes otherwise.

d. The Prevailing Challenges

Several statistics on autism and people on the spectrum have emerged, helping us further understand the disorder, its prevailing effects, and the like. This has helped in fashioning out solutions and interventions where necessary.

According to a 2020 report from the Centers for Disease Control and Prevention (CDC), approximately one in fifty-four children in the U.S. is diagnosed with ASD; furthermore, 2016 data reveal that only one in thirty-four boys and one in forty-four girls are affected by autism. Furthermore, boys are four times more on the cards to be diagnosed with autism compared to girls. Even though most children were still being diagnosed after age four, autism can be dependably diagnosed as early as age two.

About 31 percent of children with ASD possess an intellectual disability, with their intelligence quotient (IQ) averaging less than 70; 25 percent of children in this category are in the borderline range (IQ 71–85), and 44 percent have IQ scores in the average to above-average range (i.e., IQ>85). In addition, autism has been seen to affect all ethnic and socioeconomic groups, with minority groups having a greater tendency of being diagnosed later and less often. There is currently no medical detection for autism; this implies, however, that early intervention is ideal if the best support for healthy development and delivery of benefits across the lifespan is to be obtained.

e. Causes of Autism

A lot of effort has gone into research on ASD to ascertain its remote causes. A number of such researches showed that genetics are involved in the vast majority of ASD cases and that children who are born to older parents have a higher risk of contracting the disorder. Again, parents who previously had a child with ASD have a 2 to 18 percent chance of having a second child who is also affected. Studies have also shown that among identical twins, if one child has ASD, then there is a 36 to 90 percent chance that the other would also be affected; in nonidentical twins, however, the chances of the other child being affected drop to about 31 percent. In addition, far-reaching research spanning over the last two decades has enquired whether or not there is any connection between childhood vaccinations and autism; after many controversial scares, the results of this research are clear that vaccines do not cause autism.

f. Intervention and Supports

Several intervention attempts have been made; it is however worthy of note that early intervention has been seen to be most effective in bringing about improvement in learning, communication, and social skills, as well as basic brain development. Interventions such as applied behavior analysis (ABA) and an assortment of therapies based on their principles are the most researched and generally used for behavioral interventions for autism.

A lot of children affected by autism also profit from other interventions like speech and occupational therapy. Developmental deterioration, or loss of skills like language and social interests, is known to affect around one in five children who will be diagnosed with autism and typically occurs between ages one and three.

g. Autism's Associated Challenges

A great number of associated challenges continue to trial this disorder. It is estimated that 40 percent of people with autism are usually nonverbal and 31 percent of children with ASD have an intellectual disability, with an IQ averaging below 70. These suffer substantial challenges in their day-to-day function, with 25 percent in the borderline range (IQ 71–85). In addition, approximately half of those with autism wander or bolt from safety; almost two-thirds of children with ASD between the ages of six and fifteen have experienced bullying. Just about 28 percent of eight-year-olds with ASD exhibit behaviors that are regarded as self-injurious to themselves or others, with headbanging, arm biting, and skin scratching being some of the most common behaviors. Furthermore, a leading cause of death for children with ASD is drowning; it accounts for approximately 90 percent of deaths linked with drifting or bolting by those aged fourteen and younger.

h. Medical and Mental Health Conditions Associated with ASD

Typically, ASD is known to affect the entire body, with Attention Deficit Hyperactivity Disorder (ADHD) affecting a projected 30 to 61 percent of children with autism. More than half of children with ASD have exhibited one or more protracted sleep complications. Again, anxiety disorders have been known to affect a projected 11 to 40 percent of children and teens on the spectrum, while depression affects a projected 7 percent of children and 26 percent of adults with autism. Children with ASD are approximately eight times more in the cards to suffer from one or more protracted gastrointestinal disorders than are other children.

Some other conditions associated with ASD include epilepsy, with as many as one-third of people with ASD experiencing seizure disorder. Also, studies have advocated that schizophrenia does affect between 4 and 35 percent of adults with ASD; by contrast, however, schizophrenia only affects a projected 1.1 percent of the general population. Health challenges associated with ASD are spread across the life span, from young children to senior citizens, with approximately 32 percent of two- to five-year-olds with ASD being overweight and 16 percent being obese; by divergence, however, about 23 percent of two- to five-year-olds in the general population are overweight and only 10 percent are pathologically obese.

i. Caregivers, Families, and Autism Spectrum Disorder

Families and caregivers of individuals with ASD find the management of such a disorder very tasking. On average, managing autism costs a projected $60,000 per annum through childhood, with the greater part of the costs going into special services and lost wages linked to amplified demands on one or both parents. Furthermore, expenses increase with the manifestation of intellectual disability. In addition, mothers of children with ASD, who lean toward serving as their child's case manager and advocate, have been seen to be less likely to work outside the home. They typically work fewer hours per week, earning 56 percent less than mothers of children with no health challenges or restrictions and 35 percent less than mothers of children with other disabilities or disorders.

j. Autism in Adulthood

Researchers have projected that over the coming decade, a projected 707,000 to 1,116,000 teens, which is an equivalent of 70,700 to 111,600 each year, will enter adulthood and age out of school-based autism services. Teens with autism get health-care transition services half as frequently as those with other special health-care needs. Young individuals whose autism is tied to accompanying medical complications are even less probable to get transition support. Again, a lot of young grown-ups with ASD do not get any health care for years after they stop seeing a pediatrician.

A significant amount of young adults with ASD remain unemployed and unenrolled in higher education in the two years after high school. This rate is far lower than young adults in other disability groups, counting learning disabilities, intellectual disability, or speech-language impairment. People with autism who used state-funded vocational rehabilitation programs in 2014 numbered nearly 18,000; however, only 60 percent left the program having to gain meaningful employment. Of these, 80 percent worked part time at an average weekly rate of $160, putting them well below the poverty level. Approximately half of the twenty-five-year-olds with ASD have never held a paying job, and research has proven that job undertakings that encourage independence decrease ASD symptoms and upsurges daily living skills.

k. Economic Costs and Autism Spectrum Disorder

The approximate cost of caring for Americans with ASD reached $268 billion in 2015 and is projected to rise to $461 billion by 2025 in the absence of more operative interventions and support across the life span. The bulk of these costs in the U.S. are particularly for adult services, which is a projected $175 to $196 billion a year, compared to $61 to $66 billion a year for children. Averagely, medicinal disbursements for children and adolescents with ASD were 4.1 to 6.2 times greater than for those without autism.

The passage of 2014 Achieving a Better Life Experience (ABLE) Act made room for tax-favored savings accounts for people with disabilities, including ASD, to be established by states. Also, passaging autism insurance legislation in all fifty states is an inroad for provisional access to medical treatment and therapies.

l. Adult Outcomes in Autism Spectrum Disorder

Overall, outcomes in adults with ASD have been analyzed in terms of functional language, independent living, employment, and friendship/social engagement. A great number of reports do agree that the majority of adults with ASD have poor outcomes in these areas; an exception, however, is that of realization of functional language in 70–80 percent of most samples, with reports showing mostly low levels of vocational and social engagement even in connection to overall cerebral, language, and adaptive skills of a lot of adults. For instance, national survey data specified that young grown-ups with ASD had the highest rates of *no participation* in education or employment compared to those in other disability groupings appraised and that only about half the ASD cluster had held some form of paid employment within six years of high school graduation. Nevertheless, adult outcome results do contrast based on rating systems used, the chronological period of data collection and other circumstantial factors, and demographics of trials, such as IQ and age. Particular contemporary literature advocates that by taking into account person-environment suitability, outcomes may be more positive than they appear to be from objective markers of acceptability.

Previous methodical reviews, concentrating on normative measures of social outcomes in ASD, which are unbiased measures of employment, independence, social participation, and relationships, have determined that, even among partners of average intelligence, most individuals with ASD stay highly dependent on others for their care, with social contacts staying limited and employment rates remaining extremely low. Furthermore, adults with ASD are more parsimoniously, educationally, and socially underprivileged than adults with other developmental or intellectual disabilities. Twelve studies published from 1967 to 2013 indicated little change in these conclusions.

m. What You Will Get from This Book

This book seeks to enlighten the reader on various widely accepted life, social, and work skill that an adult with ASD needs to live adequately and successfully. These skills would be carefully expanded and explained such that they can be understood and applied with ease.

Each section would be accompanied by a list of activities and exercises aimed at triggering action and participation in the reader. This book isn't limited to adults with ASD alone. It also accommodates those saddled with the task of managing an individual with ASD, such as parents or caregivers, helping them gain useful knowledge that they can instill in their child or patient, helping them walk the path toward independence.

It is recommended that each section be read thoroughly and wholly absorbed before any attempt is made at implementation. Owing to the sensitive nature of the subject of ASD, any line could be misconstrued if not adequately understood. Furthermore, this book doesn't contain all the answers; so it is advised that other materials too be employed that would help buttress points made and deepen comprehension on any of the topics discussed.

CHAPTER TWO

Autism Spectrum Disorder

Autism spectrum disorder is regarded as a multifaceted developmental disorder that comprises persistent challenges in social interaction, speech and nonverbal communication, and restricted or repetitive behaviors, with the prevailing effects of the condition and the severity of its symptoms being significantly different in each person.

Typically, ASD is first diagnosed in childhood with a lot of the most obvious signs showcasing themselves around two to three years of age. However, some children with ASD do develop normally until when they become toddlers and begin to lose hitherto gained skills. Autism is a lifelong disorder, but a lot of children diagnosed with ASD do go on to live independent, productive, and fulfilling lives.

a. Characteristics of Autism Spectrum Disorders

In terms of the severity and combination of prevailing symptoms, ASD generally varies from person to person. No two individuals appear or behave the same way as there is a wide range of abilities and characteristics of persons with ASD, with symptoms going from mild to severe and often changing over time too. As a result, the characteristics of ASD fall into two broad categories:

A. Social dealings and communication difficulties

This comprises the following:

- Hitches in a normal back-and-forth conversation
- A drastic reduction in sharing of interests or emotions
- Challenges in appreciating or rejoining to social prompts such as
  o eye contact and
  o facial expressions
- Dearth in building, preserving, and appreciating relationships; trouble making friends
- Does not respond to name by nine months of age
- Does not show facial expressions such as happy, sad, angry, and surprised by nine months of age
- Does not play simple interactive games such as pat-a-cake by twelve months of age
- Uses few or no gestures by twelve months of age (e.g., does not wave goodbye)
- Does not share interests with others (e.g., shows you an object that they like by fifteen months of age)
- Does not point or look at what you point to by eighteen months of age
- Does not notice when others are hurt or sad by twenty-four months of age
- Does not pretend in play (e.g., does not pretend to "feed" a doll by thirty months of age)
- Shows little interest in peers
- Has trouble understanding other people's feelings or talking about own feelings at thirty-six months of age or older

		• Does not play games with turn-taking by sixty months of age

B.	Restricted and repetitive forms of behaviors, interests, or activities	This may comprise the following:
		• Hand flapping and toe walking or spinning self in circles
		• Playing with toys in an unusual way, such as,
		    • lining up cars, gets upset when order is changed, or
		    • tossing objects
		• Speaking inimitably, such as speaking using odd patterns or pitches or mimicking voices from favorite shows
		• Having a substantial need for an expected routine or arrangement
		• Showing penetrating interests in activities that are surprising for a similarly aged child
		    ○ Plays with toys the same way every time or
		    ○ Is focused on parts of objects (e.g., wheels)
		• Feeling the sensory aspects of the world in an uncommon or life-threatening way such as,
		    ○ unresponsiveness to pain/temperature,
		    ○ disproportionate smelling/touching of objects,
		    ○ enthrallment with lights and movement,
		    ○ being astounded by loud noises, and
		    ○ others.
		
		• Repeats words or phrases over and over (i.e., echolalia)

Most individuals with ASD have other physical characteristics. These might include the following:

- delayed language skills
- delayed movement skills
- delayed cognitive or learning skills
- hyperactive, impulsive, and/or inattentive behavior
- epilepsy or seizure disorder
- unusual eating and sleeping habits
- gastrointestinal issues (e.g., constipation)
- unusual mood or emotional reactions
- anxiety, stress, or excessive worry
- lack of fear or more fear than expected

It is essential to note that individuals with ASD may not have all or any of the behaviors listed as examples here. Another point to note is that while a lot of people with ASD have average intelligence, several others have mild or significant intellectual delays. Furthermore, people with ASD are at greater risk for some homeopathic conditions such as sleep problems, seizures, and mental illnesses.

b. Diagnosis

When it comes to the diagnosis of ASD, early diagnosis and treatment are essential, as this would help in reducing the symptoms of autism and improving the quality of life for individuals with ASD and their families. There is currently no homeopathic test for ASD; it is diagnosed based on the observation of how the child talks and acts in comparison to other children of the same age bracket. Qualified professionals characteristically diagnose ASD; they talk with the child and ask questions to parents and other caregivers.

Generally, any child assumed to have a developmental disorder can get free access to an evaluation under federal law. In addition, the American Academy of Pediatrics (AAP) endorses that children be vetted for developmental disorders at well-child preemptive visits before age three.

If a parent has apprehensions about their infant or toddler not developing normally, it is important they take their concern to their primary care provider. The Centers for Disease Control and Prevention have branded possible red flags for ASD in young children, some of which include the following:

- not responding to their name by twelve months of age

- not pointing at objects to express interest by fourteen months

- not playing "pretend" games by eighteen months

- avoiding eye contact or having a preference to be alone

- getting upset by minor changes

- flapping their hands, rocking their body, or spinning in circles

- having unusual and sometimes intense rejoinders to the way things smell, taste, feel, and/or look

If there is a robust apprehension that a child is displaying likely signs of autism, then a diagnostic evaluation should be done as soon as possible. This normally comprises an interview and play-based testing with the child carried out by a psychologist, developmental-behavioral pediatrician, child psychiatrist, or other providers.

It is a fact that scientists do not recognize what causes ASD. Several factors most likely contribute to ASD, including environmental factors or genes a child is born with. A child is at greater risk of autism if there is a family member with autism. Research has indicated that it is not caused by bad parenting, nor is it caused by vaccines.

c. Signs and Symptoms of Autism Spectrum Disorders

As stated earlier, ASD is a developmental disorder caused by dissimilarities in the brain. Many people with ASD have a known dissimilarity, such as a chromosomal condition, while for others, causes are not yet known. Scientists are certain that there are multiple causes of ASD that piece together to alter the most common ways people develop. There is still much to learn about these causes and how they impact people with ASD.

There is usually nothing about the looks of people with ASD that sets them apart from other people; they may behave, communicate, interact, and learn in ways that differ from other people. The aptitudes of people with ASD can differ considerably. For instance, some people with ASD may have forward-thinking conversation skills, whereas others may be nonverbal; some individuals with ASD need a lot of help in their daily lives, while others can work and live with little to no support.

Autism spectrum disorder shows before the age of three years and can last throughout a person's life, even though symptoms may improve. For some children, the symptoms of ASD do manifest within the first twelve months of life, while for others, the symptoms may remain undetected until twenty-four months or later. Also, several children with ASD gain new skills and meet developmental milestones, until around eighteen to twenty-four months of age when they stop gaining new skills, or they lose the skills they once had.

Today, a diagnosis of ASD now consists of several disorders that used to be diagnosed separately: autistic disorder, pervasive developmental disorder not otherwise specified (PDD-NOS), and Asperger syndrome. These disorders are now all called autism spectrum disorders. Updated criteria for diagnosing ASD comprise difficulties with social communication and interaction and restricted or repetitive behaviors or interests. It is imperative to note that some individuals *without* ASD might also have some of these symptoms. The exception, however, is that for people with ASD, these characteristics can make life very challenging for them and their families or loved ones.

d. Identification

The signs and indications of ASD can be identified by the prompt investigation, which is the collection or gathering of information and screening. Surveillance or developmental monitoring is a dynamic ongoing practice of watching a child grow and inspiring conversations between parents and providers about a child's skills and abilities. Centers for Disease Control and Prevention has come up with a program (*Learn the Signs. Act Early*) aimed at developing free materials, such as the *CDC's Milestone Tracker* app, which aids parents and providers to work together to observe the development of children and know when there might be a concern and if more screening is required.

Screening is when a parent or provider completes a checklist or questionnaire specially tailored to identify problems that need further evaluation. General developmental screening ought to be done at the ninth-, eighteenth-, and twenty-fourth- or thirtieth-month well-child visits and whenever a concern is expressed. In addition, autism-specific screening should be done at the eighteenth- and twenty-fourth- or thirtieth-month visits and whenever a concern is expressed.

e. Causes of Autism Spectrum Disorder

Scientists have established that autism spectrum disorder has no singular known cause. Given the convolution of the disorder and the fact that indications and severity differ, there are perhaps a lot of causes. However, both genetics and environment may play major roles.

i. Genetics. Quite a lot of diverse genes seem to be involved in ASD. For a number of children with an autism spectrum disorder such as Rett syndrome or fragile X syndrome, ASD can be linked with a chromosomal disorder. For other children, chromosomal mutations may increase the risk of ASD. Still, other genes may affect brain development or how brain cells interconnect, or they may define the severity of symptoms. Some chromosomal mutations seem to be genetic, while others come about extemporaneously.

ii. Environmental factors. At present, researchers are still investigating whether factors such as viral infections, medicines or impediments during pregnancy, or air contaminants play a role in triggering ASD. However, findings have shown that there is no connection between vaccines and ASD.

In the past, one of the greatest arguments in ASD centered on whether a connection exists between the disorder and childhood vaccines. Despite widespread research, no reliable study has revealed a connection between ASD and any vaccines. In fact, the original study that kindled the debate years ago has been withdrawn due to poor design and questionable research methods.

It has therefore been recommended that no childhood vaccinations should be boycotted, as doing so might place children and others in danger of getting infected and spreading fatal diseases, such as whooping cough (pertussis), measles, or mumps.

f. Risk Factors

Today, the number of children being diagnosed with ASD is on the increase. Whether this is as a result of better detection and reporting, or a real increase in the number of cases, or both remains unclear at the moment. Autism spectrum disorder affects children of all races and nationalities; however, particular factors are known to increase the risk of getting the condition. These may comprise the following:

- *The sex of the child:* Boys are about four times more probable to develop ASD than do girls.

- *Family history:* Families who previously had one child with ASD have a much higher chance of having another with the disorder. It's also not unusual for parents or relatives of a child with ASD to have slight difficulties with social or communication skills themselves or to engage in certain behaviors archetypal of the disorder.

- *Other disorders:* Children with particular medical conditions have a higher than normal possibility of having ASD or showing autism-like symptoms. Instances may comprise *fragile X syndrome*, a genetic disorder that causes cerebral difficulties; *tuberous sclerosis*, a condition in which nonthreatening tumors develop in the brain; and *Rett syndrome*, an inherited condition arising almost exclusively in girls, which causes slowing of head growth, intellectual disability, and loss of purposeful hand use.

- *Particularly preterm babies:* Babies born before twenty-six weeks of gestation may have a greater risk of ASD.

- *The age of parents:* There might exist a link between children born to older parents and ASD, but more research is needed to establish this link.

g. Complications

When an individual has complications when it comes to social interactions, communication, and behaviors, it can lead to a lot of other challenges comprising the following:

- difficulties in school and with efficacious learning

- employment difficulties

- powerlessness to live independently

- social seclusion

- pressure within the family

- victimization and being bullied

h. When to See a Doctor

Typically, babies are known to develop at their own pace, with a few not following exact timelines found in some parenting books. However, children with ASD generally display several indications of delayed development before age two. If parental concerns about the child's development or suspicion that they may have ASD arises, then a formal discussion should be engaged by the parents with a pediatrician. The symptoms linked with the disorder can also be connected with other developmental disorders.

Signs of ASD frequently show up early in the child's development when there are obvious delays in language skills and social interactions. The doctor may recommend developmental tests to ascertain if the child has delays in cognitive, language, and social skills, if the child

- doesn't react with a smile or happy expression by six months

- doesn't imitate sounds or facial expressions by nine months

- doesn't babble or coo by twelve months

- doesn't gesture by fourteen months

- doesn't say single words by sixteen months

- doesn't indulge in "make-believe" or pretend play by eighteen months

- doesn't say two-word phrases by twenty-four months

- loses language skills or social skills at any age

i. Prevention

There exist no current ways of preventing ASD; however, there are intervention options. Early diagnosis and intervention can prove to be most helpful and can improve behaviors, skills and language development in the long run. Even though children typically do not outgrow symptoms of ASD, they do learn to function adequately.

j. Categorization of Autism Spectrum Disorder

Autism is part of the five pervasive developmental disorders (PDD), which are branded by

- aberrations of social interactions and communication

- limited interests

- highly repetitive behaviors

Autism has a wide variety of severity and symptoms that is regularly used to categorize ASDs. Each of the conditions under ASD is dissimilar from the other; individuals with Asperger syndrome, for instance, do not have a substantial delay in language development. Autism itself is often called *autistic disorder, childhood autism,* or *infantile autism.* In some persons, autism may be underlying and undetected, manifesting only as a mental disability, while in others there are repetitive movements like hand flapping and rocking. Some individuals with autism may be normal in all aspects of life except for being socially awkward. They may have intently focused interests, and rambling, hair-splitting communication. Such occurrences often make boundaries between diagnostic categories a bit arbitrary due to the overlapping and myriad of features.

There is justifiably a great deal of confusion about the names of several autism-related disorders. Some professionals refer to them as *autisms* to avoid addressing the occasionally elusive variances among the disorders along the autism spectrum. Until a decade ago, there were five different ASDs, with the dissimilarities among those five being hard to grasp for parents trying to figure out which of the disorders affected their child.

The American Psychiatric Association tried to simplify matters by merging the prevalent developmental disorders into a single diagnostic classification referred to as *Autism Spectrum Disorder* in the latest edition of the diagnostic bible branded as the *Diagnostic and Statistical Manual of Mental Disorders.* As a lot of people were diagnosed prior to the change in the classification system and since a lot of experts still speak of the pre-2013 labels, they are summarized here for reference. However, for purposes of clarity, it would be stated that all of the following conditions are now incorporated under the umbrella classification *Autism Spectrum Disorder (ASD).*

The three most common forms of autism in the pre-2013 classification system were

- Autistic Disorder—or classic autism,

- Asperger's Syndrome, and

- Pervasive Developmental Disorder—Not Otherwise Specified (PDD-NOS).

These three disorders share a lot of the same symptoms, but vary in their severity and impact, with the autistic disorder being the most severe, and Asperger's syndrome, sometimes referred to as *high-functioning autism*, and PDD-NOS, or *atypical autism*, being the less severe variants. *Childhood Disintegrative Disorder* and *Rett Syndrome* were also included among the PDDs, as both are extremely rare genetic disorders and are typically well thought out to be separate medical conditions that don't truly belong on the autism spectrum.

In large part due to discrepancies in the way that individuals were classified, all of the aforementioned variants of autism are now referred to as *Autism Spectrum Disorder*. This single labeling shifts the focus away from where the individual falls on the autism spectrum to whether or not they have ASD. If a child is developmentally behind or displays other autism-like behaviors, a visit to a medical expert or a clinical psychologist who specializes in diagnostic testing would be required for a thorough evaluation. The doctor can aid in figuring out whether or not the child has ASD and how severely they are affected.

k. Neuro-Diverse Adults and Their Challenges

Autism research focused on their quality of life has gotten comparatively little attention when paralleled to the great number of autism research focused on causation. In the last several decades, more than 150,000 papers have been written about autism, with the vast majority of these papers focused on the genetics of autism, physiology, and environmental factors that may sway the trail of the neurological-developmental disability. Only a miniature portion of scholarly articles about autism in the academic literature have scrutinized real-life apprehensions currently impacting adults with ASD, such as access to critical augmentative and alternative communication (AAC), social acceptance, and compatible employment possibilities. Enhancing the quality of life of people with ASD will require that academic scholars shift their emphasis to the specific hurdles they experience.

CHAPTER THREE

Quality of Life

Quality of life is a multifaceted theory with a lot of accompanying facets. It is also an idea that depends profoundly on background and elucidation. So it is crucial to adopt an operational definition and framework. Over time, there have been wide disagreements among researchers, scholars, and professionals on how to delimit the quality of life concerning individuals with disabilities.

The World Health Organization (WHO) describes it as the perception of individuals of their position in life in the context of their beliefs and the value systems in which they live by and concerning their goals, hopes, principles, and trepidations. Quality of life is concerned with how impairment confines a person's ability to live up to a normal role. Innumerable other portrayals of the idea of the quality of life thrive in academic and professional dissertations.

However, researchers and professionals do mostly agree on the core areas that compromise the quality of life. A comprehensive review of papers on quality of life from the last three decades recognizes eight core areas and their underlying indicators:

Core Domains of Quality of Life	Indicators
Self-Determination	Autonomy, Choices, Decisions, Personal Control, Self-Direction, Personal Goals/Values
Social Inclusion	Acceptance, Status, Supports, Work Environment, Community Activities, Roles, Volunteer Activities, Residential Environment
Material Well-Being	Ownership, Financial, Security, Food, Employment, Possessions, Socioeconomic Status, Shelter
Personal Development	Education, Skills, Fulfillment, Personal Competence, Purposeful Activity, Advancement
Emotional Well-Being	Spirituality, Happiness, Safety, Freedom from Stress, Self-concept, Contentment
Interpersonal Relations	Intimacy, Affection, Family, Interactions, Friendships, Support
Rights	Privacy, Voting, Access, Due Process, Ownership, Civic Responsibilities
Physical Well-Being	Health, Nutrition, Recreation, Mobility, Health Care, Health Insurance, Leisure, Activities of Daily Living

a. Barriers to Quality of Life Experienced by Adults with Autism

i. Self-determination. Communication abilities form a crucial component of self-determination and self-advocacy for individuals, regardless of whether or not they have any disabilities. Without sufficient access to an operational means of communication, it is impossible to satisfactorily express the individual wants, needs, and predilections that attend to an individual's self-direction and decision-making. A lot of people with ASD encounter challenges with spoken language owing to cooccurring dyspraxia, which greatly sways gross and fine motor functioning and social anxiety. These individuals are likely to profit

41

greatly from having routine access to AAC systems, devices, and other forms of technologies, like letter boards, speech-generating devices, sign language, and picture/symbolic communication systems.

A handful of academic research and professional case studies have shown extensive support for the rewards of AAC in enhancing self-determination, swelling opportunities for gainful employment, and augmenting the general quality of life for people with other developmental and neurological disabilities, such as cerebral palsy and amyotrophic lateral sclerosis. People with ASD often experience a lot of the same challenges like these and other disability populations. As a result, it would imply that AAC usage could extensively enhance the quality of life of a lot of people with ASD.

However, a huge percentage of nonspeaking individuals with autism do not have satisfactory access to AAC systems, devices, or other technologies that are well matched with their distinct strengths and complications. Buying AAC systems, devices, and other technologies and paying for training on how to use them may be unaffordable for a lot of people with ASD and their families. This position is further complicated by the unambiguous exemption of AAC coverage from a lot of insurance plans owing to a prevalent fallacy that AAC has not been shown to boost the functioning of people with disabilities. People with ASD also may be perceived as not capable of benefiting from AAC owing to the predominance of speech as the major tool of communication in society, the gross underestimation of the cognitive and language abilities of nonspeaking individuals with autism, and numerous other factors.

In the same way, the methodical, logical, and detailed-oriented nature of assistive technologies, like computers and other information technologies, makes them an acceptable fit for a lot of people with ASD.

Information technologies are likely to help people with ASD in assisting them in planning and organizing their lives, in connecting socially with other people, and in participating in local community activities that often go hand in hand with self-determination. However, just as a lot of people with ASD do not have satisfactory access to required forms of AAC, they also may not have access to necessary forms of assistive technologies, like personal digital assistants (PDAs)/planners, smartphones, online communication tools, and aids for daily living.

Another foremost obstruction to the realization of self-determination for people with ASD is a central assumption held by a lot of experts that self-determination is not possible or needed for individuals with ASD. This assumption is founded upon unyielding belief systems all over the disability service-delivery community about what institutes self-determination for people with disabilities. There exists a well-known lack of understanding of the malleable and personalized nature of self-determination for people with disabilities and its connection to a person's strengths, weaknesses, preferences, values, beliefs, and goals. Given suitable support and reassurance, a lot of individuals with ASD and other people with disabilities could probably achieve a much higher level of self-determination in their daily lives than they currently do. Getting to this point, though, requires a change in communal attitudes about self-determination.

ii. Social inclusion. Ancient stigma and enduring myths and typecasts about ASD have hushed the social acceptance of people with ASD and their full inclusion in community life. A lot of condescending and debasing metaphors about people with ASD have persevered despite substantial efforts by the autistic self-advocacy and associated community to counter them. These comprise depictions of autism as a partial or whole loss of personhood, exemplifications of autism as a departure into an empty fortress, portrayals of people with ASD as being sealed inside a shell, and expositions of people with autism as victims kidnapped and held captive by their disability.

This inimical and sometimes antagonistic climate in which people with ASD find themselves has made it very hard for them to build a healthy self-esteem and to become at ease playing a part in their local communities and social gatherings. A survey of 237 adults with ASD piloted in the United Kingdom established that 83 percent of the surveyed participants with autism felt strongly or very strongly that a lot of of the utmost challenges they encountered in life stemmed directly from lack of acceptance and appreciation of their differences by other individuals with whom they worked and interrelated with regularly.

Nevertheless, when experts discuss the challenges experienced by people with ASD and other disabilities, societal stigma and attitudinal barricades on the odd occasion top the list. A lot of experts tend to emphasize their efforts on practical tasks at the expense of concentrating on the social climate surrounding disability populations. They may not be proficient in considering how social-cultural standards and perspectives form barriers in everyday life for people with disabilities.

iii. Material well-being. Underemployment is defined as an employment status where an individual's job underutilizes their skills, talents, and educational background; unemployment, on the other hand, is defined as an employment status where an individual does not have a job for an extended period. Various hypothetical studies have established that adults with ASD frequently experience huge challenges in getting and sustaining reasonable employment. These studies advocate that both underemployment and unemployment are probably much higher among people with ASD than among the nonautistic population.

This present situation matches a historical trend of much higher underemployment and unemployment among the larger community of people with disabilities. The statistical database shows that the employment rate in the U.S. of men and women aged 18–64 with an identified disability is presently around 18 percent. While underemployment is much harder to track compared to unemployment, a lot of bits of intelligence in the disability community point out that the underemployment of people with disabilities is also very common. Thus, it is logical that people with ASD, as a subset of the larger disability population, may face similar challenges in finding and maintaining jobs.

Foremost difficulties to getting and keeping employment for people with ASD that have been identified by academic studies and case reports include difficulties with the following:

- Dealing with the job-seeking and job application process: this includes developing resumes, participating in interviews, networking, and so on.

- Adjusting to new processes and routines for jobs.

- Becoming skilled at the social and communication demands of the workplace: this includes understanding job instructions, adjusting to social norms, participating in teams, and so on.

- Managing the sensory demands of the workplace.

- Engaging in goal-oriented and spontaneous thinking on the job; this includes organization, planning, and so on.

- Handling negative attitudes and stigma associated with ASD.

- Overcoming mental health challenges linked to complications at the workplace.

The perseverance of high rates of underemployment and unemployment among the autistic population points to an occupational service system that does not sufficiently deliver support for people with ASD who make an effort to work around these occupational obstacles. A recent review of the national statistics concerning the Office of Vocational Rehabilitation (OVR) services and equivalent state services established that a lot of people with ASD are in the offing to be left without access to vocational services based on a determination by experts that they are too severely disabled to profit from them. In another study, dialogues with eighteen adults with ASD found that OVR services were time and again not sufficiently set up to meet the particular needs of people with ASD; the researchers found that OVR counselors often did not have the training, resources, and background to help people with ASD in getting well-matched employment.

In addition, the disability support system likely isn't set up to coach people with ASD about their right to reasonable accommodations in the workplace. A 2008 study of employment discrimination grievances advocated that only a very small percentage of people with ASD file discrimination complaints when they are denied necessary accommodations under the ADA. The study also gathered that discrimination complaints by people with ASD constituted only .003 percent of all ADA complaints filed for a given year. However, people with ASD represent a much larger percentage of the general population (over 1 percent by many estimates) and an even larger proportion of the community of people with disabilities.

Another major barricade to material well-being experienced by people with ASD is the lack of compatible housing and living options. Quite a few longitudinal studies have advocated that a large percentage of people with ASD may be living with their parents, in institutions, or developmental centers rather than in apartments, houses, and community living. Another recent study on the daily living situations of seventy-four adults with ASD in the Andalusia province in Spain showed that 87 percent of the participants were living at home with their parents. This present state came about from a lack of focus on creating sufficient housing options for adults with ASD and other people with disabilities who would decide on living away from home if given the option.

A lot of people are certain that living away from home automatically involves independent living in an apartment or house. This only embodies one possible housing option for adults with ASD. The development of housing supports for adults with ASD requires tractability and a wide variety of other options, including apartment-style shared disability communities, stand-alone apartments existing on the property of a family home, vocational communities where workers at the same company live together, homes operated by a microboard, and many other options.

iv. Personal development. One of the foremost obstacles to personal development for people with ASD is a lack of suitable support resources during postsecondary education. Postsecondary education comprises the pursuit of studies past high school at career and trade schools, two-year colleges, and four-year colleges and universities, as well as studying for professional certifications. There exist only a trivial number of universities and colleges that have established specialized programs for students with autism in the United States, some of which include Marshall University, Western Kentucky University, Fairleigh Dickson University in New Jersey, the University of Arizona, the University of Alabama, Oakland University in Michigan, and Keene State College in New Hampshire.

Students with ASD who go to colleges and universities other than these schools will repeatedly find nominal disability accommodations and services, such as extended time on tests that may not sufficiently support some of the trials they face in such areas as planning and organizing their studies, fitting into the social-cultural atmosphere of a college campus, founding and sustaining friendships and social relationships, living in a dorm, and managing the sensory and motor skill demands of college.

Even students who do attend the institutions listed above may be incapable of participating in their specialized autism support programs owing to restricted enrolment sizes and high costs. All of the specialized support programs have limited enrolment and program fees, aside from school tuition that often exceeds $4,000 per annum. When combined with tuition, room and board, and course expenses minus the cost of acquiring books and project materials, the cost of these specialized support programs may be excessively high for many college students with autism, particularly bearing in mind that the cost of higher education for all college students has risen progressively in recent years.

Another obstruction to the pursuit of postsecondary education for people with ASD is the shortage of support for individuals with ASD who decide on pursuing vocational and trade school opportunities. No academic studies or books have been issued precisely about people with ASD at vocational and trade schools. There exists a deficiency of studies and books about the experience of vocational and trade schools for people with disabilities in general.

v. Emotional well-being. Quite a lot of research studies have shown that mental health debilities may come about more frequently among adults and adolescents on the autism spectrum than among the nonautistic population. A review conducted in 2006 comprising twenty-seven academic papers on depression and autism established that the rate of depression among people with ASD might be 34 percent or higher.

An earlier appraisal of several case studies on depression and autism acknowledged a 41 percent pervasiveness of depression among people with ASD. Furthermore, the study also established higher rates of other mental health disabilities among the autistic adult population, including bipolar disorder, anxiety, obsessive-compulsive disorder, and schizophrenia. In addition, raised rates of anxiety-related disabilities among people with ASD, including social anxiety, generalized anxiety, separation anxiety, panic disorder, and agoraphobia were also found. All of these mental-health-related disabilities may likely have an enormous impact on daily living, employment, community participation, and social acceptance of people with ASD.

Nevertheless, there subsists a general lack of adequate resources and training related to mental health disabilities and people with ASD. There are hardly any professional guides and handbooks that have been published on subjects concerning mental health disabilities and people with autism in the past decade. A lot of counselors and mental health service providers may not have satisfactory training for working with clients with ASD, and they may not have partaken in any recent professional expansion in the autism field. In the same way, a lot of providers of services to people with autism may not have adequate training in mental health disabilities.

vi. Interpersonal relations. *Development in interpersonal relations during adulthood consists of cultivating friendships, romantic relationships, and other social relationships. Various difficulties and strengths in language, communication, and social interaction form a major feature of the disability of autism. As a result, it means that individuals with ASD are probably going to face difficulties in forming and maintaining social relationships. Several academic studies submit that this is the case; however, there exists a deep dearth of resources for assisting adults with autism to circumnavigate social relationships. Most* *support resources in the autism community related to social relationships center in detail on children with autism and young adolescents.*

While online social interaction may help adults with autism develop social relationships, online-only relationships do not allow for engaging in shared activities and recreation with friends, such as going on group outings (e.g., bowling, concerts, sporting events, festivals, and parades, etc.), eating together, volunteering as a group, and mutually supporting each other. Consequently, developing programs to support people with autism in navigating face-to-face social interaction is essential. Likewise, developing a base of academic studies about both face-to-face and online social interaction for people with autism is necessary.

In addition, individuals with ASD may also face difficulties in pursuing romantic relationships. Even though there exist few or no academic articles about romantic relationships for persons with ASD, personal accounts by people with autism do show that learning how to develop such relationships and traverse dating and marriage may be most challenging for a lot of them. This problem may be further aggravated by communal opinions that romantic relationships are not necessary or achievable for people with ASD.

These assessments correspond to inequitable attitudes toward people with other developmental and neurological disabilities. Individuals with intellectual and developmental disabilities generally have encountered discriminatory practices by members of society to thwart their partaking in romantic relationships and to border their ability to have children. For example, people with intellectual disabilities generally went through procedures to neuter them during the early 20th century. More than 47,000 forced sterilizations of people with intellectual and developmental disabilities in thirty states occurred in the four-decade span between 1907 and 1947. Even though such obligatory sterilization for any other subcategory of the population is very rare in the 21st century, undesirable attitudes and out-of-date views concerning romantic relationships for people with intellectual and developmental disabilities have even so continued. These biases have often limited the ability of people with ASD to take part in romantic relationships of their choosing.

vii. Rights. The United Nations embraced the Convention on the Rights of Persons with Disabilities in 2006 and endorsed the document in 2007. More than one hundred countries are signatories to the convention, including the United States. The general principles and obligations toward people with disabilities adopted in the convention apply as much to the population of people with ASD as they do to other disability population groups. The general principles include the following:

1. Respect for the dignity, autonomy, and independence of people with disabilities

2. Nondiscrimination

3. Full and effective participation in society

4. Respect for differences and acceptance of persons with disabilities as part of human diversity

5. Equality of opportunity

6. Accessibility

7. Equality between men and women

8. Respect for the evolving capacities of children with disabilities and respect for the right of children with disabilities to preserve their identities (UN, 2007)

Even though these fundamental rights delineated by the UN convention should be available to all adults with ASD and other disability population groups, the reality is that a lot of these rights are not available to people with autism. In particular, principles A, B, C, and D are often not observed:

1. People with ASD, every so often, do not find respect for their dignity, autonomy, and independence in society, including the media.

2. People with ASD may experience frequent discrimination by people who seek to malevolently take advantage of their challenges.

3. People with ASD, time and again, are not full participants in their local communities and greater society.

4. People with ASD frequently do not find respect for their differences, and their disability is not seen as a part of human diversity.

viii. Physical well-being. Lack of supportive recreational and physical activity programs remains a foremost obstacle to the realization of healthy physical well-being by adults with ASD. Researchers in 2004 found that adults with ASD who experience major challenges in social interaction and communication may be less probable to participate in organized recreational programs with high social hassles, as those programs may not admit and understand their differences. As a result, adults with ASD may become secluded from the community and may center their amusements wholly on solo hobbies regardless of potential interests in partaking in community recreational activities. This situation often becomes enfranchised as a false belief that all persons with ASD have a strong distaste for partaking in social recreational opportunities, a misunderstanding that may then discourage community organizations from altering their recreational programs to enable people with ASD to participate.

Another possible obstacle to physical well-being is the dearth of understanding and acceptance of adults with ASD in the health-care system. While health-care providers and agencies may be educated about children with ASD, they may understand very little about adults with ASD. This may make it very perplexing for adults with ASD to access health-care services when needed. Other obstacles to accessing and using the health-care services may include filling out forms, navigating the social norms of the health-care environment, and managing the sensory demands of health service facilities.

CHAPTER FOUR

Living with Autism Spectrum Disorder and Other Special Needs

The term *special needs* is an umbrella term used to refer to a wide assortment of diagnoses, from those that resolve swiftly to those that will be a challenge for life and those that are comparatively mild to those that are profound. Persons with special needs may have developmental delays, medical conditions, psychiatric conditions, and/or genetic conditions. These special needs often necessitate accommodations so that individuals can reach their potential. Regardless of the reason, the special needs label is beneficial, as it can help the person access needed services, set suitable goals, and gain an understanding of the person's situation and the pressures their families may be under.

a. Definition and Categories of Special Needs
A clear definition and an understanding of the various categories of special needs can help one in dealing with occurrences as they come and when they involve individuals with special needs. Having it at the back of one's mind that certain people may behave in certain ways due to their disabilities and that there are laws that will protect them from discrimination and intimidation can assist with how this category of people should be approached, engaged, and related with. Special needs are well defined as a term used to label individuals with mental,

emotional, or physical disabilities. Typically, an individual with special needs may require assistance with the following:

- communication

- movement

- self-care

- decision-making

There are several types of special needs included, all of which affect the efficient functioning of an individual in a number of critical ways. Some are genetic, others are due to certain environmental factors, while the causes of others remain unknown. However, they all have one thing in common; they all cause delays in the mental, physical, or psychological development of the individual:

- Autism

- ADHD

- Cerebral palsy

- Down syndrome

- Emotional disturbance

- Epilepsy

- Reading and learning disabilities

- Intellectual disabilities

- Pervasive developmental disorder

- Speech and language impairments

- Spina bifida

- Traumatic brain injury

- Visual impairments

Generally, individuals with disabilities or special needs may require distinctive care, and to make certain of their safety, a number of laws have been enacted into government.

b. Challenges and Triumphs

One of the major drawbacks of the descriptions of special needs is that they generally relate to what a person *can't* do, such as unmet marks, prohibited foods, must-be-avoided activities, or unattainable experiences. These limitations can affect families immensely, making special needs look like an awful designation. Furthermore, a number of parents may continue to mourn the lost potential of their kids, with other conditions becoming more disturbing as time passes. Other families may find that the challenges of their child make conquests sweeter and that feebleness is often escorted by astonishing strengths.

Exercise

Respond to the following questions as honestly as you can.

1. How have you perceived the label, "Special need"?

_____

_____

_____

_____

2. *How has the designation impacted you or your child in the advancement of their lives generally, whether positively or negatively?*

_____

_____

_____

_____

3. *Do you feel this form of generalization of the term helps the individuals in the community of people with disabilities, and why?*

_____

_____

_____

_____

c. Each Family Has Different Concerns

It is truly a fact that sampling two families of individuals with special needs will always lead to the conclusion that they may appear to have little in common. A family whose main concerns are centered on the developmental delays of their child would have dissimilar priorities and apprehensions than the family dealing with a protracted ailment. Even so, both families would have dissimilar worries compared to other families whose concerns are centered on managing mental illness, learning problems, or behavioral challenges. This explains why special needs are seen as a very broad term, with every situation being unique. It is often recommended that families should focus on looking for the help and direction necessary for their specific concerns.

Exercise

Respond to the following questions as honestly as you can.

1. *What have been the main concerns for you and your family as regards your unique special needs?*

_____

_____

_____

_____

2. *How is this different from the concerns of other families that you might know who also have a person with special needs?*

_____

_____

_____

_____

i. Medical issues. Medical problems for children comprise serious conditions like cancer, heart defects, muscular dystrophy, and cystic fibrosis. It also includes chronic conditions such as asthma and diabetes, congenital conditions like cerebral palsy and dwarfism, and health threats like food allergies and obesity. A kid with special needs may require recurrent medical testing, hospital stays, equipment, and accommodations for disabilities. It is often recommended that a robust support system should be put in place when dealing with uncertainties and any medical crises.

Exercise

Respond to the following questions as honestly as you can

1. What has been the main medical challenge for you and your family as regards your unique special needs?

_____

_____

_____

_____

2. How has a robust support system helped you in the management of your ailment?

_____

_____

_____

_____

ii. Behavioral issues. For children with behavioral issues, traditional disciplinary measures often do not work for them. Diagnoses such as ADHD, fetal alcohol spectrum disorder, dysfunction of sensory integration, and Tourette's syndrome necessitate tailored approaches that are custom made to their exact needs. Behavior issues come with a lot of undesirable results, such as an increased likelihood of problems at school. It is often recommended that parents be more flexible, creative, and patient.

Exercise

Respond to the following questions as honestly as you can.

1. What have been the main behavior challenges for you and your family as regards your unique special needs?

_____

_____

_____

_____

2. *How has adopting a tailored approach to managing your disability helped in your general behavioral improvement?*

_____

_____

_____

_____

3. *How has a robust support system helped you in the management of your ailment?*

_____

_____

_____

_____

iii. Developmental issues. It is a fact that one's visions of the future and plans to make provision for abrupt complications in caring for and educating one's child can be affected by developmental disabilities. Diagnoses such as ASD, Down syndrome, and intellectual disabilities every so often cause people to be removed from the mainstream, which in itself, affects the general development of the individual. For developmental complications, tailored approaches are usually the best and are often recommended; however, they come at a steep price. This is why we see parents often come to become stern advocates to make sure their children get the services, therapy, schooling, and inclusion they need and deserve.

Exercise

Respond to the following questions as honestly as you can.

1. *What have been the main developmental challenges for you and your family as regards your unique special needs?*

_____

_____

_____

_____

2. *How has adopting a tailored approach to managing your disability helped in your general developmental improvement?*

_____

_____

_____

_____

3. *How has a robust support system helped you in the management of your ailment?*

_____

_____

_____

_____

iv. Learning issues. Learning disabilities such as dyslexia and auditory processing disorder (APD) cause affected individuals to struggle with schoolwork irrespective of their intellectual capabilities. They typically necessitate focused learning approaches to meet their potential and avoid self-esteem complications and behavioral difficulties. Parents of kids with learning challenges require a lot of persistence; this comprises working with the child at home as well as teachers and schools to make sure they get all the help they need.

Exercise

Respond to the following questions as honestly as you can.

1. *What have been the main learning challenges for you and your family as regards your unique special needs?*

_____

_____

_____

_____

2. *How has adopting a tailored approach to managing your disability helped in your general learning improvement?*

_____

_____

_____

_____

3. *How has a robust support system helped you in the management of your ailment?*

_____

_____

_____

_____

v. Mental health issues. Coming to terms with the fact that one's child suffers from anxiety or depression or has attachment complications can be astonishing. Even though every child will be different, it generally can leave families dealing with a roller coaster of mood swings, crises, and defiance. It is often recommended that parents find the right professionals for assistance. In addition, they may also need to make decisions about therapy, medications, and, possibly, hospitalization.

Exercise

Respond to the following questions as honestly as you can.

1. *What have been the main mental health challenges for you and your family as regards your unique special needs?*

_____

_____

_____

_____

2. *How has adopting a tailored approach to managing your disability helped in your general mental health improvement?*

_____

_____

_____

3. *How has a robust support system helped you in the management of your ailment?*

_____

_____

_____

_____

Even though every individual with special needs is different and every family is unique, some common apprehensions connect parents. These comprise getting proper care and encouraging acceptance in the extended family, school, and community. For some, planning for an ambiguous future may be obligatory. They will also find themselves regulating routines and expectations, occasionally quite often. Out of need, parents or caregivers of individuals with special needs are often more flexible, compassionate, stubborn, and resilient than other parents. While it may not be something previously hoped for or expected, it is important for the person's sake that the best foot is put forward by all parties concerned.

d. Significant Special Education Laws

Scholars with disabilities and special needs may require exclusively planned and methodically delivered teaching techniques. Special education programs work to help individuals cultivate not only their academic abilities but also the personal skills that aid them in becoming self-reliant members of the community.

Historically, in the United States, special education programs became mandatory in 1975 to prevent discrimination by public educational institutions against individuals with disabilities. Today, the National Center for Education Statistics reports that, as of 2013, just about 13 percent of all students in public schools were receiving special education services.

i. Education for All Handicapped Children Act. This piece of legislation was passed by Congress in 1975; it was the first special education law focused on students with physical and mental disabilities. The law itemized that public schools must afford children with special needs the same chances for education as other children. It also obligates any public school that receives federal funds to make available one free meal a day for these children.

The undertaking of this act was to

- make special education services easily reached to children who need them;

- maintain fair and suitable services for disabled students;

- introduce methodical evaluation requirements for special education; and

- award federal resources to public schools for the education of disabled students.

ii. Individuals with Disabilities Education Act. The Individuals with Disabilities Education Act, or IDEA, was fashioned in 1990 and is an amendment of the Education for All Handicapped Children Act. This law guarantees that students with special needs take delivery of suitable free public education in the tiniest obstructive environment needed to meet those students' necessities. It aids students in getting the added support they need but then lets them take part in the same activities as children without special needs.

iii. No Child Left Behind Act. The Elementary and Secondary Education Act, commonly known as the No Child Left Behind Act, was enacted in 2001. Congress called for schools to be answerable for the academic performance of all students, whether or not they had disabilities. The act necessitates schools in every state to develop routine assessments of the academic skills of students. Even though it does not specify that these assessments meet a national standard, the law indulges each state to come up with its measures for evaluation. No Child Left Behind delivers incentives for schools to demonstrate progress in students with special needs. It also lets students seek other options if schools are not meeting their academic, social, or emotional needs.

iv. Individualized education programs. The IDEA upholds that parents and teachers of children who are eligible for special education must develop an Individualized Education Program, or IEP, that aids in forming specific education for a child's unambiguous needs. This necessitates initial meetings by caregivers to conclude a child's eligibility for an IEP and to come together once a year to develop and assess the educational plan.

The student's educational strategy must be selected in writing and should include an evaluation and description of the current academic status, measurable goals, and objectives, description of an instructional setting and placement within that setting, and transition services for children aged 16 or older. An IEP offers parents the right to dispute any issues with the school district through an unbiased third party.

v. Students with disabilities and postsecondary school. While the Rehabilitation Act of 1973 and the ADA of 1990 are aimed at forbidding discrimination based on disability in schools, this policy applies to colleges and universities as well as elementary, middle, and high schools. A lot of students with special needs go on to study at the postsecondary level; however, the laws are somewhat different for postsecondary schools. The law does not necessitate postsecondary schools to provide a free suitable public education to students; nevertheless, it does indulge schools to offer suitable academic modifications and accessible housing to students with disabilities.

Thorough knowledge of special education laws is important for students with disabilities or for individuals looking to teach children with disabilities. These laws preserve the rights of students and their families, aiding in integrating students with special needs into society without any form of segregation. Even though the laws vary slightly from state to state, the acts passed by Congress assist in standardizing the treatment of students with special needs across the country.

Exercise

Respond to the following questions as honestly as you can.

1. *How many of the laws mentioned above are you or your child conversant with?*

_____

_____

_____

_____

2. *Which of the aforementioned laws has worked for you or served to the immense benefit of your child or patient and how?*

_____

_____

3. What amendment would you prefer to see in the nearest future that has to do with these laws?

_____

_____

_____

_____

e. Difficulties Faced By People with Disabilities

It is normal for every person to encounter challenges that reveal the limit of our human nature. Facing and conquering challenges reinforces the fact that humans are indeed nature's greatest creation. Here are a few challenges and difficulties faced by people with disabilities, how they deal with them, and what could be done to make their lives a bit happier:

i. Accessibility. People with physical disabilities, like every other person, would need to navigate their way through spaces, and they typically have to do so using wheelchairs or crutches. However, the way most living spaces or environments are crafted does not take into account the limitations of people with disabilities. This means moving around freely is not a luxury that a lot of them can afford, as a lot of public places today are rarely made with the comfort of people with disabilities in mind. Little or no provisions are made for ramps, or hallways are designed too narrow for them to move. Thankfully these days, a lot of wheelchairs are automated, and buildings are being constructed with private residential elevators tailored to make the movement of disabled people a little bit easier.

Exercise

Answer the following questions as honestly as you can.

1. *Have you had any challenges with access to any of the city's public or private buildings? If yes, what kind of challenge was it?*

_____

_____

_____

_____

2. *What are some of the things you have suffered due to challenges relating to deficits in accessibility?*

_____

_____

_____

_____

3. *What areas of accessibility deficits would you like to see fixed in your community in the nearest future, and why?*

_____

_____

_____

_____

ii. Education. The fact remains that education is a basic right for all humans and ought to be free and available to everyone in an ideal world; however, this is hardly the case. A sizable number of children with disabilities remain out of school, thus depriving them of their right to basic education and cutting them short of the privilege of running life's race like their neurotypical kids. To overcome this challenge, quite a lot of educational institutions have been established, primarily focused on the education of these individuals with special needs, from teaching the Braille system to adaptive technology, which aids them in leading better lives.

Exercise

Answer the following questions as honestly as you can.

1. *Have you had any challenges with education in your city of residence? If yes, what kind of challenge was it?*

_____

_____

_____

_____

2. *What are some of the things you have suffered because of challenges in education?*

_____

_____

_____

_____

_____

3. *What areas in your education would you like to see fixed in your community in the nearest future, and why?*

_____

_____

_____

_____

iii. Access to health care. To say the least, the health-care system in America today is already very stretched, as it serves a large number of people. Poor people do not have access to adequate health care and people with disabilities are worse off. Every so often, people with intellectual disabilities are maltreated by health workers, and this makes matters even worse. This can be only addressed by appropriate awareness and understanding. People with disabilities deserve all the medical care that is legally affordable to them and should be treated with the utmost care. Consequently, it is demanded that everyone should donate to ensure NGOs are able to provide for their health-care needs in a much better way.

Exercise

Answer the following questions as honestly as you can.

1. *Have you had any challenges with health care in your city of residence? If yes, what kind of challenge was it?*

_____

_____

_____

_____

2. *What are some of the things you have suffered because of poor health-care services in your community?*

_____

_____

_____

_____

3. *What areas of health care would you like to see fixed in your community in the nearest future, and why?*

_____

_____

_____

_____

iv. Myths and stereotypes. For some reason, there remains a dark conformist nature in our culture that appears to have stuck with us like a leech. One part of it is the issue of myths and stereotypes targeted against people with disabilities. This isn't restricted to communities, ethnicities, or races; it thrives all over the world howbeit regrettably. When people interact with other people with disabilities, they fall victim to certain myths that stem out of their dearth of knowledge and compassion toward such people.

Exercise

Answer the following questions as honestly as you can.

1. *Have you been a victim of myths and stereotypical references in your city of residence? If yes, what kind of challenge was it?*

_____

_____

_____

_____

2. *What are some of the things you have suffered due to some myths and steretypes held by people in your community?*

_____

_____

_____

_____

3. *What myths and stereotypes would you like to see busted/broken in your community in the nearest future, and why?*

_____

_____

_____

_____

*v. **The feeling of being ignored**.* Oftentimes, when people interact with other persons with disabilities, they generally conclude that such persons are incapable of a lot more than they already are, such that interacting with a person who has problems walking, for instance, could make one feel they also have hearing or visual challenges. This thought process often stands in the way of effective interaction and communication with such people, with the person with a disability left with deep feelings of being ignored or undermined. These disability barriers need to be brought down, which is only possible with more awareness.

Exercise

Answer the following questions as honestly as you can.

1. *Has your disability been misunderstood, which leads to being ignored or undermined? If yes, what was it?*

_____

_____

_____

_____

2. *What are some of the things you have suffered due to being ignored or undermined in your community?*

_____

_____

_____

_____

3. *What would you like to see corrected in your community in reference to being undermined in the nearest future, and why?*

_____

_____

_____

_____

vi. Lack of employment. Typically, the employment of any resident should be predicated upon their education and skills that they acquired up along the way. However, when people with disabilities suffer from unemployment due to a lot of reasons ranging from discrimination to a lack of basic education, it is bound to make them fall behind other candidates for that job. Thankfully, the government has come up with various schemes that help guarantee jobs for people with disabilities.

Exercise

Answer the following questions as honestly as you can.

1. *Have you had a challenge with gaining employment in your city of residence? If yes, what kind of challenge was it?*

_____

_____

_____

_____

2. *What are some of the things you have suffered due to employment discrimination in your community?*

_____

_____

_____

_____

3. *What areas of employment for people with disabilities would you like to see fixed in your community in the nearest future, and why?*

_____

_____

vii. The feeling of being incompetent. In a lot of cases, people with disabilities require more time to do a particular task compared to other people. This is because the barriers brought about by their disability prevent them from performing basic tasks with ease. This invariably gives the wrong impression to other members of the team that the person with disabilities is pulling them down. As much as this might be the case in reality, the fact remains that the competence of the persons with disabilities isn't below par and shouldn't be dismissed.

Exercise

Answer the following questions as honestly as you can.

1. *Have you had any challenge with the feelings of being incompetent in your city of residence? If yes, what kind of challenge was it?*

_____

_____

_____

_____

2. *What are some of the things you have suffered due to a poor perception of your ability to handle or perform a task in the workplace?*

_____

_____

_____

_____

3. *What areas in your workplace would you like to see fixed with reference to the feeling of being incompetent in the nearest future, and why?*

_____

_____

_____

_____

viii. Teased and abused. Every so often, people find gratification in putting others down; they somehow find dominance in bullying the weak and disadvantaged. People with disabilities often find themselves at the receiving end of such violent and disgusting actions. Even though schools and institutions taking bullying very seriously and have crafted out antibullying policies to safeguard the vulnerable members of their community, this act remains one thriving misnomer that ought to be addressed.

Exercise

Answer the following questions as honestly as you can.

1. *Have you been a victim of teasing or abuse in your city of residence? If yes, what kind of challenge was it?*

_____

_____

_____

_____

2. *What are some of the things you have suffered due to teasing, abuse, or bullying in your community?*

_____

_____

_____

_____

3. *What areas would you like to see fixed in your community in the nearest future in reference to teasing and abuse, and why?*

_____

_____

_____

_____

ix. Being patronized. People with special needs find themselves being patronized often by others who feel that's the best way to express sympathy. They every so often hear things like, "*I know what you are going through*" or "*I know this must be hard.*" Patronizing people with disability with words such as these never do justice to the difficulties they encounter and go through every day. The fact remains that a person is likely not to know exactly what a person with a disability is feeling.

Exercise

Answer the following questions as honestly as you can.

1. *Have you been a victim of patronization in your city of residence? If yes, what kind of challenge was it?*

_____

_____

_____

_____

2. *What are some of the things you have suffered as a result of you constantly being patronized in your community?*

_____

_____

_____

_____

3. *What areas would you like to see fixed in your community in the nearest future in reference to the unacceptable patronization of people with disabilities, and why?*

_____

_____

_____

_____

x. Relationships. The human race is a complicated one, where people judge themselves and others on a set of factors that may or may not apply to all circumstances. Such predispositions fundamentally affect relationships, leading to mistrust and misunderstanding. The majority of people with disabilities struggle to find love, friendship, and companionship; this often brings sadness and loneliness in their lives.

Exercise

Answer the following questions as honestly as you can.

1. *Have you had challenges with relationships because of your status as a person with a disability? If yes, what kind of challenge was it?*

_____

_____

_____

_____

2. *What are some of the things you have suffered due to difficulties in relationships with people in your community?*

_____

_____

_____

_____

3. *What areas would you like to see fixed in your community in the nearest future in reference to enhancing relationships, and why?*

_____

_____

_____

_____

A lot of the aforementioned issues can be handled if people become more thoughtful and have patience when dealing with people with special needs. Work should be made available for people with special needs; this will give them financial independence and arrange for satisfaction in their life. In addition, our surroundings should be fashioned in such a way that they can be more accessible to people with special needs.

Also, residences for people with disabilities should be designed in such a fashion that they are more comfortable for these people. In addition, one can always lend a helping hand to people in their moment of need, no matter how small the contribution is.

CHAPTER FIVE

Life Skills

Life skills as defined by WHO are abilities for adaptive and positive behavior; these abilities empower individuals to effectively handle and manage the demands and challenges of everyday life. Another definition provided by the United Nations International Children's Emergency Fund (UNICEF) states that life skills are premeditated behavioral changes or behavior development methods to tackle a balance of three fundamental areas, namely knowledge, attitude, and skills. This description is predicated on investigative proof that advocates that changes in risk behavior are not likely to occur if knowledge, attitudinal, and skills-based competency are not handled.

In essence, life skills are those abilities that assist in promoting the mental well-being and competence of young people as they encounter the realities of life. Most development experts agree that life skills are generally functional in the context of health and social events, which can be applied in many content areas such as HIV/AIDS and drug use prevention, sexual violence, teenage pregnancy, and suicide prevention. This description further encompasses consumer education, environmental education, peace education or education for development, livelihood, and income generation, among other things. In summary, life skills empower young individuals to take affirmative actions aimed at protecting themselves and promoting their health and social relationships.

Life skills do describe a set of rudimentary skills which could be assimilated through learning or direct life experience, enabling individuals and groups to meritoriously manage issues and problems generally encountered in daily life. Such skills comprise creativity, critical thinking, problem-solving, decision-making, the ability to communicate and work in partnership, along with personal and social responsibility that add to good citizenship.

Life skills touch upon issues that are

- tangible, having the propensity to affect people's lives.

- topical.

- occasionally sensitive; they can move people on a personal level, particularly when family or friends are involved.

- often controversial; people disagree and hold strong opinions about them.

- ultimately moral; they relate to what people think is right or wrong, good or bad, and important or unimportant in the social order.

a. The Requirements for Teaching Life Skills

Today, our societies are in need of people who are keen on taking responsibility for themselves and their communities, contributing to the political process. People who can impact teachings on various subjects, including life skills must possess the following, among other things:

- be cognizant of their rights and responsibilities as citizens,

- be knowledgeable about social and political issues,

- be concerned about the welfare of others,

- be able to plainly articulate their opinions and arguments,

- be able to influence the world,

- be active in their communities, and

- be responsible in how they act as citizens.

While a few life skills may be assimilated via our everyday experience in the home or at work, they are not satisfactory enough to sufficiently prepare a person, particularly individuals with ASD or other special needs for the active role required of them in today's complex and diverse society. If a person is to become frankly involved in public affairs, then a more systematic approach toward life skills education is needed.

b. The Benefits of Training in Life Skills

- It aids in the development of self-confidence and effectively dealing with important life changes and encounters, such as bullying and discrimination.

- It gives voice to the voiceless at schools, in communities, and the societies at large.

- It facilitates the formation of positive contributions by the development of the needed proficiency and experience required to affirm rights and understand duties while getting ready for challenges and opportunities of adulthood and work life.

c. Core Life Skill Strategies and Techniques

Various international bodies such as UNICEF, United Nations Educational, Scientific and Cultural Organization, and WHO came up with a list of the ten core life skill strategies and techniques that are required to be assimilated; they include problem-solving skills, critical thinking, effective communication skills, decision-making, creative thinking, interpersonal relationship skills, self-awareness building skills, empathy, and coping with stress and emotions.

Self-awareness, self-esteem, and self-confidence are critical tools for appreciating one's strengths and weaknesses. As a result, the individual can detect available occasions and get ready to face likely threats. This leads to the growth of social awareness of the apprehensions of one's family and society. Then, it is conceivable to recognize problems that arise within both the family and society.

With life skills, a person is able to discover options, weigh pros and cons, and make balanced decisions in resolving every problem or issue as they arise. It also involves being able to create prolific interpersonal relationships with others. In addition, life skills allow effective communication, for instance, being able to distinguish between hearing and listening and ensuring that messages are conveyed correctly to avoid miscommunication and misconstructions.

d. Components of Life Skills
Life skills are categorized into three main components. According to WHO, they include the following:

i. Critical thinking skills/decision-making skills. These consist of decision-making/problem-solving abilities and information gathering skills. In addition, the person must also be accomplished at appraising the future consequences of their present actions and the actions of others. Again, they would also need to be able to decide on alternate solutions and to examine the influence of their ideals and the ideals of those around them.

ii. Interpersonal/communication skills. These consist of verbal and nonverbal communication, active listening, and the aptitude to express feelings and give feedback. In addition, negotiation/refusal skills and assertiveness skills that directly affect the person's ability to manage conflict must be learned. Empathy, which is the ability to listen to and understand the needs of others, is also an important interpersonal skill. The cultivation of an important skill set such as teamwork and the aptitude to cooperate, as well as conveying respect for those around us, helps the individual to get accepted in society. These skills end in the acceptance of social norms that afford the basis for adult social behavior.

iii. Coping and self-management skills. These talk about skills that upsurge the internal locus of control so that the person believes that they can make a difference in the world and bring about change. Self-esteem, self-awareness, self-evaluation skills, and the ability to set goals are also part of the more general category of self-management skills, with the ability to manage anger, grief, and anxiety and learning to cope with losses or traumas. Stress and time management are important, as are positive thinking and relaxation techniques.

Generally, the life skills approach is projected to succeed if the following are embarked on together:

1. The skills. This consists of a collection of psychosocial and interpersonal skills that are interwoven with each other. For instance, decision-making would probably involve creative and critical thinking components and value analysis.

2. The content. The effective way of behavior is determined by the utilization of skills in a specific content area. Learning about decision-making will be more evocative if the content is pertinent and remains continuous. Such content areas could be labeled as drug use, HIV/AIDS/STI prevention, suicide prevention, or sexual abuse.

Whatsoever the content area, an equilibrium of three elements needs to be well thought out, namely *knowledge, attitudes, and skills.*

3. The methods. Skills-based education cannot come about when there is no interaction among contributors. It relies on groups of people to be effective. Interpersonal and psychosocial skills cannot be assimilated from sitting alone and reading a book. If this approach is to succeed, all three components—life skills, content, and method—must be in place. This meritoriously implies that life skills can be learned via the use of specific methods and tools.

e. Criteria for Using Life Skills

The following criteria warrant a successful life-skills-based education:

- It should not only tackle changes in knowledge and attitude but, more essentially, changes in behavior.

- Desired changes in attitudes and behaviors are typically not achieved exclusively by traditional information-based approaches, as these are not sufficient. For instance, a lecture on *safe behavior* will not automatically breed the practice of *safe behavior.* As a result, the lecture should be corroborated with exercises and circumstances where participants can practice safe behavior and experience its effects. The adult learning model stresses that adults learn best if they can associate what they are learning with their experience and practice.

- Learning typically would work best when amplified or reinforced. If a message is given once, the brain generally recalls only 10 percent of it one day later, and when the same message is reiterated six times a day, the brain remembers 90 percent of it. Therefore it is necessary to repeat, recap, reinforce, and review.

- Learning would work best if pooled with policy development, access to appropriate health services, community development, and media.

f. How Life Skills Help With Making Better Choices

Developing life skills aids adults in interpreting knowledge, attitudes, and ideas into healthy behaviors, like getting the ability to lessen special health risks and embrace healthy behaviors that improve their lives in general, such as career planning, decision-making, and forming positive relationships. Today, young people grow up encircled by sundry messages about sex, drug use, alcohol, and adolescent pregnancy. On one hand, parents and teachers caution about the dangers of early and promiscuous sex, adolescent pregnancy, STDs/HIV/AIDS, drugs, and alcohol; on the other hand, messages and behavior from entertainers and peer pressure challenge those messages, with them even frequently promoting the opposite behavior. It is through life skills that teenagers can contest these challenges and safeguard themselves from teenage pregnancy, STDs, HIV/AIDS, drug violence, sexual abuse, and many other health-related complications.

With any luck, developing life skills among young people will empower girls to avoid pregnancy until they reach physical and emotional maturity, develop in both boys and girls responsible and safe sexual behavior, sensitivity and equity in gender relations, get boys and young men ready to be responsible fathers and friends, inspire adults, particularly parents, to listen and rejoin to young people, help young people avoid risks and hardships, and include them in decisions that affect their lives.

Programs meant for the development of life skills have fashioned effects such as diminished violent behavior, amplified prosocial behavior, and diminished negative self-destructive behavior.They have also augmented the ability to plan and decide on effective solutions to problems, value-added self-image, self-awareness, social and emotional adjustment, improved acquisition of knowledge and classroom behavior, brought about improvements in self-control and management of interpersonal problems and coping with nervousness, and enhanced constructive conflict resolution with peers, instinct control, and acceptance.

Recent studies have also revealed that sex education based on life skills was more effective in conveying changes in adolescent contraceptive use, deferral in sexual debut, deferment in the onset of alcohol and marijuana use, and in developing attitudes and behavior required for preventing the spread of HIV/AIDS.

g. Seven Essential Life Skills

The seven essential life skills are given below:

1   Focus and self-control

2   Perspective-taking

3   Communication

4   Making connections

5   Critical thinking

6   Taking on challenges

7   Self-directed, engaged learning

i. Focus and self-control. A lot of individuals with ASD and other forms of special needs do grow well on schedules, habits, and routines. These schedules not only generate feelings of security but also aid people with ASD to learn self-control and focus. Scheduling would involve talking to the person about what to expect each day and helping them organize their living or working space such that they know where to put shoes, coats, and personal belongings. Since we are surrounded by a noisy, distraction-filled world, quiet activities such as reading a book, enjoying sensory activities, or completing a puzzle can help the person to slow down and increase focus.

The skill of *focus and self-control* is particularly important today as we do our best to get everything done each day, having it in mind that life today can be stressful. Studies endorse that individuals with this skill are more in the offing to learn from educational experiences and practice, have better academic achievement, graduate from college, and experience better health and economic prosperity in adulthood.

Focus and self-control consist of executive function skills, including focus or paying attention, working memory or recollecting what we need to know so that we can use the information, cognitive flexibility or thinking adaptably so that we can retort to the changing situations in our lives, and inhibitory control or resisting a reflex response so that we can think before acting and choose a more suitable response.

1. Promoting focus and self-control. Ideally, this skill, and others such as it, is best cultivated when an individual is very young. As much as adults too can learn these skills, it is often much more difficult to inculcate it in adults than it is to do in children. So it is recommended that such pieces of training and teachings be initiated from a very early age. Be that as it may, it is important to add that as much as it is difficult to groom this skill in adults, it is not impossible or unattainable; so any person with ASD or other forms of special needs can be encouraged to learn, regardless of their age.

Below are some research-based ways to help improve children's focus and self-control:

Everyday Routines

- It should be common practice to indulge your children or young adults with games that involve paying attention to details, such as 'I Spy' to practice focus. So when fixing dinner, folding the laundry, or waiting in line at a store, play games with them.

- When cleaning up any space, you can boost attention by holding up an item or toy and encouraging the young adult to find similar ones to put away.

Playful Learning Activities

- When singing a familiar song together with your child or young adult, pause and leave out a word so that the child can use their working memory to add the missing word.

- When reading or telling a story to your child or young adult, encourage them to predict what might happen next; this will help them with paying careful attention and deep thinking.

- You can help practice self-control by playing games that involve "*stop*" and "*go,*" such as Red Light, Green Light or Musical Chairs.

- You can dance slowly to fast music and then quickly to slow music. This will help your child develop focus and employ self-control.

Learning Strategies

- If you or an individual with ASD or special needs is constantly being confronted by certain things, like changes or taking turns, you can encourage them to come up with their plan for how to handle the situation. By so doing, you promote the development of self-control.

- It is important to be encouraged or keep encouraging the person to keep trying when they make an error; this will aid them in learning that making mistakes is a natural part of learning.

Exercise

Answer the following questions as honestly as you can.

1. *What have been your concerns about your focus and self-control or that of your adult with ASD or special needs?*

_____

_____

_____

_____

2. *What are some of the daily activities that have helped you improve focus and self-control?*

_____

_____

_____

_____

3. *What other games or exercises have you participated in that have helped you improve focus and self-control?*

_____

_____

4. What other strategies have you applied that have helped you immensely in promoting focus and self-control?

_____

_____

_____

_____

ii. Perspective-taking. For a lot of individuals with ASD or special needs, thinking about another's point of view doesn't come naturally; nonetheless, it can be developed. Perspective-taking is the active scrutiny of the psychological experiences of others; it is a great tool for conflict resolution, designing human-centered products, and being a better leader. Empirical studies have indicated that it has many positive impacts, from upsurging team creativity to reducing implicit bias. All that is required is the visualization of someone else's worldview.

Perspective-taking goes far beyond fellow feeling; it comprises seeing things as others would see them—their likes, dislikes, feelings, and thoughts. It embroils executive function skills, together with working memory or recalling how others may react, inhibitory control or constraining our judgments to appreciate the perspectives of others, cognitive flexibility or observing circumstances in dissimilar ways, and reflection or bearing in mind the thoughts and feelings of others. Perspective-taking surfaces in children over time; however, it requires constant encouragement. Young adults with perspective-taking skills are expected to adjust better to school, to understand what they are learning through reading and writing, and to build positive relationships with fewer conflicts.

1. The four-step perspective-taking technique
Seek Understanding

Typically, when two people are communicating with each other, their instincts make them inclined toward considering their personal goals. This first step of perspective-taking encourages the mindful decision of setting one's individual goals aside. In its place, the perspective of the other party is brought to the center. Letting go of one's ego, they decide instead to employ their lived experience and the way they are perceiving the world.

Allow Ideas

In this step, one imagines numerous possibilities, working through the common obstacles to perspective-taking. Then, navigations are made around such obstacles to further see the other person clearly and imagine how they might be thinking about a situation. Even though these are assumptions and may not be accurate, however they're as close one can get to the truth.

Theorize

Now that a few ideas have been formulated, one can now narrow their thoughts down to best guesses. These can serve as solid hypotheses which can be tested and used to connect with the other person. If such a hypothesis is accurate, one can expect a certain type of outcome, and if things go wrong, it can be seen or known.

Observe and Adjust

The final step would require that one holds their hypothesis lightly, engages with the other party, observes, and adjusts laid down assumptions. One has to opt for an open discussion, stay curious, and be ready for insights. The needed breakthrough would surface once a connection and collaboration are established. If this is not the case, a deeper and further challenge to one's assumptions would be needed. Whatever the result, the process of perspective-taking doesn't end. It's a constant cycle of empathy, imagination, estimation, and discovery.

2. Promoting perspective-taking. Here are a number of research-based ways to aid in the improvement of perspective-taking:

- Intentionally put aside your feelings; this will help you focus only on the other person's perspective.

- Do not come at the situation with a mission in mind. It is best to always approach with curiosity.

- Employ the use of open-ended questions; this will help in drawing out the interests of the other person that they may not be verbalizing.

- Be clear about your position and the downside it has.

- Remove any personal intentions; this will help avoid projecting them on the other person.

- Use what you know about the person in imagining how they would see the current situation; use their background, their mood, their intentions and expectations, and so on.

- Once you have a grasp of their perspective, try to predict what their reaction will be; this can help adjust your responses, moving them toward the outcome you desire.

- Validate their position even if you don't agree with it; do this by rewording back to them what you think their position is.

- Use the mirroring technique, imitating actions, postures, and facial expressions to put them at ease and form a connection.

Everyday Routines

- During the day, you can encourage the child to talk about their thoughts and feelings and make out how these vary from what others might think and feel. By doing so, they are practicing perspective-taking.

Playful Learning Activities

- When reading or storytelling, you can ask the child or young adult open-ended questions about a character such as, "How do you think he feels? Why do you think he feels this way?" This will help them appreciate the character's perspective.

- You can also encourage the child or young adult to express thoughts and feelings through acting out stories, telling stories, making art, or dancing.

Learning Strategies

- Encourage the child to listen to others describing their thoughts and feelings about a shared experience.

- Assist the child in learning to use words to express their feelings; also, encourage them to use this approach instead of physically acting out.

- Deliberate on ways to solve a conflict with other people; encourage the child to seek the help of an adult.

Exercise

Answer the following questions as honestly as you can.

1. *What have been your concerns about your perspective-taking skill or that of your adult with ASD or special needs?*

_____

_____

_____

_____

2. *What are some of the daily activities that have helped you improve perspective-taking?*

_____

_____

_____

_____

3. *What other games or exercises have you participated in that have helped you improve perspective-taking?*

_____

_____

_____

_____

4. *What other strategy have you applied that has helped you immensely in promoting perspective-taking?*

_____

_____

iii. Communication. Individuals with ASD or other forms of special needs require high-touch personal interactions every day to build healthy social-emotional skills, together with the ability to understand and communicate with others. Even though the speed at which they develop these skills may differ, they, nevertheless, need to learn how to read social cues and listen judiciously. They must reflect on what they desire to communicate and the most effective way to do so. This skill can be greatly improved by just talking with an interested adult, spending time every day listening and responding to without distractions, amongst other things.

Communication skills continue to develop as they grow and learn. It involves executive function skills, such as focusing or paying attention to define what we want to communicate, cognitive flexibility or thinking about how our communications will be understood by others, and inhibitory control or switching what we want to say for another way of expressing ourselves, particularly if our previously chosen approach isn't the most effective way.

1. Habits for improving communication skills. Here are five habits that better one's communication skills:
Ask questions

Effective communication comprises listening just as much as it is about talking. When someone is speaking, it is critical to take note of things they are saying, and this doesn't have to be done with a notebook and pen. A good way to do this is by asking critical questions about what the other person is saying. When you identify parts of the conversation you want to know more about and ask follow-up questions, you build better communication.

Use defined vocabulary

Having a more defined vocabulary will help improve one's communication skills. It is important not to leave any room for misinterpretation when you speak. Make it a habit not to say things that you think the other person wants to hear, and don't say things that you won't stand by. Always say what you mean, and mean what you say. You will be able to communicate your ideas much more clearly when you use precise language and don't waffle on what you mean.

Use body language

Body language is a remarkable tool that aids in communication. The human body is usually very good at communicating on its own. Still, if you desire better communication skills, then recognizing what types of body language will help you express yourself is important. For instance, try to avoid crossing your arms when having a conversation, as this can make you seem closed off, and not open to new ideas. Another way to use body language is to imperceptibly copy the person with whom you're speaking; this helps put the other person at ease and develop a rapport.

Listen

Listening is fundamental when it comes to becoming a better communicator. A lot of people confuse *listening* with *hearing.* Generally, we *hear* what others say, but *listening* involves *taking in* what's being said. You have to be sensitive to the emotional state of the person talking, recognizing the things they are saying and *not* saying. It's central to learn how to listen if you want improved communication skills. In the end, you need to be able to respond accurately after listening.

Acknowledge first; speak second

Part of good communication skills is always acknowledging what has been spoken before taking the opportunity to speak. For instance, you can say, "*Yes, I hear what you're saying...*" and then go on to speak. Better still, acknowledge explicit parts of what was said to show that you've been utilizing your listening skills. "*I understand that...*" or, "*So what you're saying is...*" Not only will the other person feel they have been heard, but they will likely listen to what you have to say as well. Part of the objective in communication includes making the other person want to listen to you as much as they want to speak.

2. Promoting communication. Here are some research-based ways to help children improve the life skill of communication:
Everyday Routines

- During the day, act as a sportscaster, and narrate what you are doing so that the child or young adult can attach words and meanings to everyday experiences.

- Employ the use of rich and diverse language; if you speak more than one language, use that, too.

Playful Learning Activities

- Ask the child or young adult to go over an experience by making a drawing or telling a story.

- You can help the child identify and label pictures in books.

- Play a sport or game where the child has to respond appropriately to what others do in the game.

- Ask the child to act out characters to tell a story.

Learning Strategies

- You can embolden the child to think about what they want to communicate, taking cognizance of how others will react to what they say.

- You can have the child listen to others and practice to and fro conversations where they take turns talking.

Exercise

Answer the following questions as honestly as you can.

1. *What have been your concerns about your communication skill or that of your adult with ASD or special needs?*

_____

_____

_____

_____

2. *What are some of the daily activities that have helped you improve communication?*

_____

_____

_____

_____

3. *What other games or exercises have you participated in that have helped you improve communication?*

_____

_____

4. *What other strategy have you applied that has helped you immensely in promoting communication?*

_____

_____

_____

_____

iv. Making connections. True learning comes about when one can see connections and patterns between apparently incongruent things. The more connections one makes, the more sense and meaning one makes of their world. Children begin to see connections and patterns as they arrange basic household items such as toys and socks. Simple acts, like choosing clothing suitable for the weather, help them form connections. Parents can help by pointing out more intangible connections in life, or in stories, such as, *"This book reminds me of when we picked seashells at the beach."*

The life skill of making connections is fundamental to learning. The ability to make connections triggers the ability to see that symbols, like numbers, letters, and words, can have symbolic representation. Making connections encompasses executive function skills, including working memory or drawing on what you know, cognitive flexibility or figuring out what's the same and what's different, and inhibitory control or sorting these things into categories.

All children and adults must explore this core component of creativity, which is to improve their capacity to make usual and unusual connections.

1. Promoting making connections. Here are some research-based ways to help improve the skill of making connections

Everyday Routines

- You can take advantage of mealtime for making connections. Ask the child how many people will be at dinner, and therefore how many forks or napkins they would need on the table. Do so alongside showing them the symbol for that number.

- While getting dressed, ask the child to select two pieces of clothing and figure out a number of ways in which they are similar and all the ways they differ.

- When you go out for a walk, ask the child to point to three things they see, then ask what the similarities between them are. Keep going and find new things that are alike and different; this is a great way to learn how to make connections.

Playful Learning Activities

- You can pen down words as the child says them so that they see the connection between what they say and what is written.

- You can ask the child to play sorting games; they can put big things in one pile and small things in another pile. You can alter the rules, and sort by colors.

- You can play "guess that song." Clap the rhythm of a song, and ask children to guess what the name of the song is.

Learning Strategies

- You can embolden the child to ponder on why they made a mistake and what they can learn from it. This can aid the child in reflecting on the connections they are making in learning.

Exercise

Answer the following questions as honestly as you can.

1. *What have been the challenges for you or that of your adult with ASD or special needs as regards making connections?*

_____

_____

_____

_____

2. *What are some of the daily activities that have helped you improve making connections with others?*

_____

_____

_____

_____

3. *What other games or exercises have you participated in that have helped you in making stronger connections?*

_____

_____

4.   *What other strategy have you applied that has helped you immensely in promoting connections with others?*

_____

_____

_____

_____

v. Critical thinking. The complexity of life daily requires adults to analyze information and make decisions about countless things; this means that critical thinking is one skill that cannot be ignored. Developing critical thinking skills is an advantageous practice for everyone, as the skill serves well in school, university, at work, and in life. Critical thinking skills can be cultivated; in fact, they can become unconscious within us, beginning with small steps.

Building critical thinking can be done via rich, open-ended activities and play. When growing up, make sure your child has time each day to play alone or with friends. Plays such as role-playing, (pretending to be firefighters or superheroes), Lego structure building, board games, or outdoor physical games like tag or hide-and-go-seek are good for the development of the skill. Via play, children formulate hypotheses, take risks, try out new ideas, make mistakes, and discover solutions.

This life skill is the constant quest for valid and reliable knowledge to guide opinions, decisions, and actions. Critical thinking comprises executive function skills, including working memory or using what you know to search for information, cognitive flexibility or seeing information in new ways as you seek to expand your understanding, and inhibitory control or not going with the spontaneous and reverting to archaic information but using the information you have obtained. Critical thinking is crucial in making sense of the world and being a problem solver. It trails an evolving path, emerging in children over time, but its use must be encouraged.

1. Essential habits needed for critical thinking.
Explore Questions

By asking questions, one can get the mind thinking on a deeper level. Critical thinkers frequently ask a lot of questions. This applies to everything from easy household tasks such as deciding on a clothing color to making a substantial financial choice, such as buying a property.

Questions help in the development of one's mindset, which primes us for tackling more bulging and in-depth questions.

Nevertheless, critical thinking also includes knowing both how and where to look to find the answer. Critical thinking begins with thinking about something that needs to be known.

- What are you curious about?

- What do you want to know more about?

- Why do things happen this way? How can I get better?

Whatever the case, it involves the art of asking questions and locating the information being sought after. Asking questions triggers habitual curiosity and helps one to learn more about one's subject of interest.

Strengthens Weaknesses

Even though everyone has strengths and weaknesses, our weaknesses can always be enriched. Naturally, one will encounter difficulties while trying to improve one's weakness, but it's no reason to give up. For instance, becoming a better listener, communicator, or eating healthier would entail taking small steps. The easier the steps, the more the lessons will stick. Whatever needs to be improved upon must be approached with critical thinking, with the recognition of one's weaknesses, making an improved proactive plan, and then acting on it.

Solve Problems Daily

Critical thinking naturally leads to problem-solving as problems are understood to be part of life. The aptitude to solve problems critically is a necessary skill, as problems employ us in disciplined critical thinking. No matter the size of the problem, one's mind can profit from solving a problem each day. The more one gets familiar with solving problems, the more they train their brain and think better.

Learn Something New Everyday

There will always be something new to learn, and the act of learning never stops. Being a learner for life does keep the mind renewed and young. It is one of the most indispensable critical thinking habits to have. There are myriad different ways to experience learning in life, from learning something in a random conversation, a breaking news story, to a book, or anything that intrigues us. Still, merely getting information isn't learning. You have to combine it with action. To strengthen what is learned, one has to practice and play with the new skills.

One of the best ways to reinforce learning into the brain is to teach what has been learned to someone else.

2. Promoting critical thinking. Here are some research-based ways to help improve critical thinking:
Everyday Routines

Use a problem-solving process to aid the child with everyday difficulties, like a fight among friends:

- *State the problem*: "When you got upset with your friend, you didn't like it and your friend didn't like it either."

- *Involve the child in coming up with solutions*: "What ideas do you have that would help you calm down when you get upset?"

- *Have children list ideas*: "Write down some ideas on how to act whenever this kind of situation arises."

- *Evaluate each solution:* Ask the child to reflect on whether or not it would work for them and the adults.

- *Pick one to try:* See if it works; if it doesn't, reserve punishment or judgment, and meet again to identify a new solution.

Playful Learning Activities

- You can both take turns telling an adventure story with a twist; once the story is underway, say, *"Oh no. There's a problem!"* Share what the problem is and appreciate what imaginative and thoughtful solutions the child comes up with.

- You can invite the child to play pretend games where they act as detectives and have to solve thrillers.

Learning Strategies

When the child asks a question in which they could figure out the answer, don't answer right away. Instead, encourage them to pursue the answer for themselves; this will spark their curiosity and critical thinking.

- Say "I wonder how we can find out the answer to that question?" and see if the child has ideas.

- If they don't have ideas, you can offer guidance by asking questions, setting up an experiment, looking in a book, or on the Internet together.

- Ask them to appraise their answers rather than telling them it is right or wrong. Come up with answers together.

Exercise

Answer the following questions as honestly as you can.

1. *What have been the challenges for you or that of your adult with ASD or special needs as regards critical thinking?*

_____

_____

_____

_____

2. *What are some of the daily activities that have helped you improve critical thinking skills?*

_____

_____

_____

_____

3. *What other games or exercises have you participated in that have helped you with critical thinking?*

_____

_____

_____

_____

4. *What other strategies have you applied that have helped you immensely in promoting critical thinking?*

_____

_____

_____

_____

vi. Taking on challenges. One of the most significant qualities to develop is that of resilience; the ability to take on encounters, bounce back from disappointment, and keep trying. Children learn to take on challenges when the enabling environment with the right amount of structure is created. Embolden your child or young adult to try new things and allow reasonable risk, like climbing a tree or riding a bike. Propose a new challenge when they appear ready, for instance, say "*I think you're ready to learn to tie your shoes. Let's give it a try.*" Emphasize effort, not an achievement. Say, "*Learning to tie your shoes was hard, but you kept trying. Well done.*"

It is a fact that all adults and children will profit from this life skill by learning how to manage stressful circumstances proactively. It involves executive functions, comprising inhibitory control or not going with the instinctive but rather reflecting on the experience or situation and cognitive flexibility or being flexible in thinking about solutions to the problem.

Children who take on trials instead of circumventing or merely coping with them realize better in school and life.

1. Promoting taking on challenges. Here are some research-based ways to help improve the life skill of taking on challenges:
Everyday Routines

- You can pick peaceful moments to help the child plan for what to do when tense. You can try to create a story together that includes ideas for how the child can handle these challenges, such as creating a fun song to sing when saying goodbye. Then try out the plan when things get nerve-wracking.

Playful Learning Activities

- When making art, embolden the child to continue creating something even if it isn't working out the way they hoped. Assist them in coming up with approaches that can solve their problem, such as painting over something they don't like with white paint and starting again.

- You can help the child manage their emotions if they lose a game by reminding them that doing their personal best is the real win.

Learning Strategies

- You can encourage the child to ask a trusted person for assistance with handling a tough situation.

- You can explore joint problem-solving. Talk with the child about what has worked in the past when they're trying something tough to help them figure out what might work this time.

- You can encourage the child to appreciate that attitude matters. Retell them when they're stressed that the essential thing is to continue learning and improving, not necessarily doing things right.

Exercise

Answer the following questions as honestly as you can.

1. *What have been the challenges for you or that of your adult with ASD or special needs as regards taking on challenges?*

2. *What are some of the laudable achievements you encountered due to taking on challenges?*

3. *What other activities and games have you participated in that bordered around taking up challenges?*

_____

_____

_____

_____

4. *What other strategy have you applied that has helped you immensely in taking up challenges?*

_____

_____

_____

_____

vii. Self-directed, engaged learning. Any individual with ASD or other forms of special needs who loves learning will become an adult who is hardly bored in life. Parents and caregivers can encourage the love for learning by trying to limit television while buoying up plenty of reading, play, and open-ended exploration. In addition, parents can exemplify curiosity and enthusiasm for learning by visiting the library together with the young adult, keeping craft supplies, making games available, and allowing for some messes at home.

Setting goals and strategies for learning nurtures the inherent curiosity of the individual to learn and aids them in better preparing for the changes as the world around them changes. After all, it's through learning that we can attain our potential. This life skill involves the executive function skills comprising inhibitory control or not going on the spontaneous but instead pondering upon the experience or situation and setting goals and working toward them and cognitive flexibility or being flexible in thinking about how to learn something in a new way.

1. Promoting self-directed, engaged learning. Here are some research-based factors that matter in improving self-directed, engaged learning:

- You can help the child in establishing trusting relationships that promote learning, as relationships are the fuel of learning.

- You can help the child in working toward their own goals or wishes, starting with a probe of what interests them.

- You can embroil the child in learning in ways that draw on their social, emotional, and cognitive aptitudes. Children learn best when they're fully engaged.

- You can help deepen and extend the child's learning by widening their thinking and offering new experiences and information that build on their interests.

- You can help the child practice, blend, oversimplify, and share what they have learned to bring together different ideas and use what they have learned.

- You can help the child become more and more responsible for their learning by fashioning safe spaces where they can learn in ways that build on their strengths, instead of concentrating on weaknesses.

- Create a community of learners, and exemplify your learning by sharing something new or how you've learned from a mistake.

Exercise

Answer the following questions as honestly as you can.

1. *What have been the challenges for you or that of your adult with ASD or special needs as regards engaged learning?*

_____

_____

_____

_____

2. *What are some of the laudable achievements you encountered due to engaged learning?*

_____

_____

_____

_____

3. *What other activities and games have you participated in that bordered around engaged learning?*

_____

_____

_____

_____

4. *What other strategy have you applied that has helped you immensely in deepening your learning?*

_____

_____

CHAPTER SIX

Life Skills—Safety Awareness

Safety skills last a lifetime and are essential to survival. Individuals with ASD grow up to become adults who live in and give back to their communities, just like all other persons. Even though some safety threats become less of a concern as kids get older, new safety threats come to the burner, taking on different forms. Even adults on the spectrum who live, work, and socialize self-sufficiently are still susceptible to certain blind spots, particularly in unaccustomed circumstances. However, skills which they master during childhood and adolescence, in the long run, serve as the base for safety and personal fulfillment in adulthood. This emphasizes the significance of beginning early and practicing often.

Safety skills build on each other and allow your individuals with ASD or other forms of special needs to navigate more complex threats successfully with age. These kinds of threats cut across environments and are the hallmark of adulthood. An artless misunderstanding can quickly twist out of control, with substantial health, legal, and financial implications. This can appear overpowering and even frightening, but being aware of what to expect can help with anticipatory planning. Granted, these individuals will falter as they go, making mistakes along the way, particularly during the years of transition when they will probably be trying to balance the need for independence with the need for support. Parents and caregivers can always help by guiding their loved ones into safe thinking, encouraging them to always have a plan in place, building a safety network such as relatives, friends, and mentors, and becoming capable self-advocates.

a. Community Safety

Adults with ASD may know how to successfully move around certain places, such as their neighborhood, as they have practiced and are familiar with people and places in their daily lives. When an individual on the spectrum is expected to function in unaccustomed locations or travel for any number of reasons, keeping personal safety can be more challenging, particularly if the individual has not had occasions to take a broad view of the skills they have learned. Adults with ASD need to be equipped to get around safely, understand the basics of travel and transportation routes, and apply safety skills in new settings.

Here are some helpful threat deterrence tips:

- Parents need to teach travel safety basics during childhood and adolescence years. Make family holidays an occasion for learning; this will help make your loved one comfortable with the process of traveling, whether by car, train, airplane, or other means. Furthermore, it will help them know how to search for information from trusted sources irrespective of the destination.

- Adults with ASD should be encouraged to research any known travel destinations carefully in advance, even if it is just an unfamiliar location in their hometown. This will help them in feeling more comfortable and confident. This is particularly central as appearing lost or confused can upsurge the probability of being besieged or taken advantage of.

- The individual with ASD should be taught how to call for safety in case of an emergency. When lost, been stalked, followed, or when confronted by danger, they should be taught how to call for safety. The following should be taught to the individual with ASD.

- How to reach the police and fire safety officers via cellphone; their city code should be memorized.
- How to use pepper spray; this should be taught with extreme caution.
- How to use a rape whistle.
- Hand signals to indicate that they are in danger and need help.
- How to break a fire alarm glass in case of a fire.
- How to use a fire extinguisher.
- How to carry out cardiopulmonary resuscitation and stop bleeding.

Exercise

1. *What challenges have you encountered as a result of not observing community safety tips?*

_____

_____

_____

_____

2. *When the aforementioned challenges occurred, what would you have done differently?*

_____

_____

_____

_____

3. *What other safety practices have you employed over the months and years that have helped you immensely?*

_____

_____

_____

_____

b. Financial Safety

With greater independence comes greater contact with all the common pitfalls. How to handle one's finances and financial information is important for community safety, as individuals with ASD who seek to be independent would have to be capable and comfortable with using money, understanding its value, and saving it. Financial safety concerns in adulthood often orbit around gullibility or too much trust; this is also often the case for adults with ASD. Your loved one with ASD must be aware of specific personal information that must be protected, like their Social Security number, bank account information, Internet passwords, and so on. The adult must understand the risk posed by identity theft and be taught to recognize schemes and scams that could come in the form of electronic mail from strangers asking for financial information (phishing), phone calls from people they don't know asking for personal information, or more of late, impromptu cold calls from unknown persons to someone's home or apartment. Sometimes the caller might say a bill is unpaid, a relative is stranded and needs money, or that they have just won the lottery, all intended to get the person to provide their credit card or bank account number.

Here are a few tips to help your loved one with ASD about finances:

- Give them a basic grasp on financial subjects. Familiarize them with the basics, and make sure they can explain in simple ways if approached with questions.

- Start early. Begin with the basic money skills such as identifying different denominations of currency, then move onto things like addition and saving. For younger children, you can teach them to drop bills and coins into a piggy bank, and for older children, have them sort money by type and value, add up the amounts, and talk about the importance of saving.

- Use real money and situations when possible. Young adults with ASD need to be able to associate what they are learning with the real world. If the money you are using to teach doesn't look like what they have been practicing with, they may become muddled in a real-world setting, and thus get irritated.

- Work to establish an allowance. No matter how trivial, stipends teach your child the importance of work and give them the chance to take possession of their own money. Be sure to keep it consistent, and pay the same amount in the same denominations on the same day each week.

- Teach the value of what money can (and can't) buy. You can play *store* at home and count out money in exchange for goods. If your child has an allowance, have them pay for something they want with their own earned money. This is a great occasion to talk about why they can and cannot afford certain things and to teach the significance of spending smart.

- Set up a bank account. If you can, set up an appointment and take your child with you to the bank to let them make their deposit each month. Talk to them about simple banking terms: deposits, balances, interest, debit cards, etc. If your child doesn't do well in a bank setting, online banks are a great option you can make use of.

- Utilize special interests. Your child or young adult with ASD almost certainly has a special interest in something. Whether it is dinosaurs, a video game, or a portion of favorite food, try and integrate it into whatever you are doing. For instance, get a piggy bank that guises like a favorite character, or talk about saving up for something they love.

- Teach long-term vs. short-term goals. Once you open a bank account for them, use the occasion to teach long-term versus short-term goals and delayed gratification. Set financial goals for money in your child's bank account, whether for a new camera or a video game system. In addition, you can buy tiny minuscule shares in a company that makes products they love to teach them about an investment.

- Help them comprehend credit and debt. Once your child turns eighteen, set up a simple store credit card that is paid off every month to help them start establishing credit. This radically increases their access to independence in the future since jobs, apartments, and even car insurance is looking for a good credit score. Founding healthy credit habits early set them up for success in the long run.

Exercise

1. *What challenges have you encountered as a result of not observing financial safety tips?*

_____

_____

_____

_____

2. *When the aforementioned challenges occurred, what would you have done differently?*

_____

_____

_____

_____

3. *What other financial safety practices have you employed over the months and years that have helped you immensely?*

_____

_____

_____

_____

c. Law Enforcement Safety

Individuals with ASD are more likely to intermingle with law enforcement than their characteristic peers and that ensues for any number of reasons. On one hand, perhaps a behavior is misunderstood, such as a lack of eye contact or not being able to communicate verbally, they have been mistreated, or they need some other type of public safety support, such as from wandering away. On the other hand, the person with ASD may have unintentionally misjudged a circumstance in a public setting. Either way, the person with ASD must recognize that police officers and first responders may not know anything about autism and have no way of identifying a person with autism by simple observation.

With that in mind, there are a lot of ways to make such interfaces go effortlessly. While more and more law enforcement agencies are providing their personnel with some autism awareness training, it is also good practice for adults on the spectrum to appreciate the role of law enforcement and first responders, and know how to properly interact with them.

Here are some helpful tips to avoid major mix-ups:

- Get to know local law enforcement personnel. Adults with ASD can practice interacting with them early and often. This might include visiting the station and familiarizing oneself. Idyllically, the footing for this would have been laid down during similar meetings in adolescence and by role-playing apt behaviors and specific types of circumstances in which your loved one might need to be in contact with an official.

- Know when to disclose. The adult with ASD should have an autism diagnosis disclosure plan in place and understand how significant it is in emergencies or happenstances with law enforcement personnel. In addition to having a clear and thought-out disclosure statement, it might also be beneficial to have an ID card or perhaps an information card about autism to help explain.

Exercise

1. *What challenges have you encountered as a result of not observing law enforcement safety tips?*

_____

_____

_____

_____

2. *When the aforementioned challenges occurred, what would you have done differently?*

_____

_____

_____

_____

3. *What other safety practices have you employed over the months and years that have helped you immensely?*

_____

_____

_____

_____

d. Relationship and Sexual Safety

Every relationship has a usual movement and different sets of apt interactions. Although the cognitive and social development of an individual with ASD may not be at par with their physical development, they will have the same sexual urges and feelings that their peers have. Therefore, sex education is just as essential for this population. Your loved one with ASD most probably has been practicing relationship safety skills and social skills training throughout their life. While adolescents may have trouble appreciating the difference between an acquaintance and a friend, adults may have trouble traversing more nuanced relationships with coworkers, colleagues, or romantic partners. Adults with ASD are more prone to misunderstandings and misconstructions, which can sometimes lead to undesirable consequences. For instance, a young man on the spectrum may show interest in a young woman at a social event, but she does not give back this interest. If he does not pick up on her body language or verbal cues and stay away, she may perceive his behaviors as harassment or even stalking. Also, it can be hard for adults with ASD to know what information is fitting to share or do publicly as opposed to privately.

Relationship safety is erected on direct instruction, practice, and experience in relationships. Appreciating different relationship types, how relationships grow, and applying anticipations for relationships often starts in adolescence. While your adult with ASD might need ongoing support such as practicing fitting behaviors and discussions for different kinds of relationships, underpinning the difference between what information is public and what should be kept private, and so on, investing that time and energy will go a long way toward keeping them safe later in life.

While the conversations about sexuality during adolescence mostly spins around the changing body and understanding or controlling urges, the conversation about sexuality in adulthood incorporates more multifaceted, interpersonal variables, such as satisfying desires, partnership, and love. These can form trouble spots for adults with ASD, even though they may have a fairly developed understanding of what sex involves from an anatomical perspective. Most remarkably, they are at a higher risk of being taken advantage of. Contemporary research shows that adults with ASD when asked about their engrossment in unwanted sexual experiences, report at least one occurrence of victimization than adults without ASD, i.e., 78 percent compared to 47.4 percent of adults without ASD.

Though it might be a very bumpy topic, it is vital to make sure that your loved one is able to define if and when they are being victimized. Your earlier conversations with them about defining what it means to be a friend will surely apply here, but the conditions and language are different when sex is involved. Be direct about what harassment or even rape entails, and give them tactics for how to get out of an unwelcome or potentially dangerous situation.

e. Strategies for Improving Sexual Safety

Every child or adult, whether or not they have an ASD, needs to learn practical information and skills related to puberty and body changes, different types of relationships, modesty and appropriate public behaviors, and other aspects of human sexuality. For preteens and teenagers on the spectrum, it is vital that assumptions not be made about what they know or will pick up intuitively, or about their level of understanding of what they are hearing and seeing. Here are some general strategies concerning what, where, how, and when to teach your young adult with ASD:

- Because of the high possibility of sexual abuse for people with ASD, lower functioning adults must be taught how to take care of their bathing and hygiene necessities themselves.

- It is imperative to teach your preteen about puberty before their body begins to develop. Or else, a girl may think she is bleeding to death when she has her first period, and a boy may think he is *wetting the bed* when he has his first wet dream.

- Usually, teens with ASDs are emotionally less mature than their peers. They may not be prepared for some information about

127

intimacy and sexuality, but they will need to have some sexuality education to lessen the possibility of acting inappropriately or being sexually abused. Furthermore, children who are mainstreamed will hear their peers chat about the subject and would need to be aware of what it all means.

- All teenagers need to know about cleaning and dressing, but if the young child is mainstreamed, they would have to be taught much more about grooming, dressing, and styles, and why these areas are so essential to their peers. Fitting in is an essential skill that is central for self-esteem as well as for future success in the world of people without ASD. At the very least, teens on the spectrum must look neat and clean, but having an item or two of *cool* clothing will help them fit in even more. Fitting in may also reduce the chances of being bullied. This, however, doesn't suggest that the teen loses their identity or preferences nor does it suggest perpetually mimicking others in a bid to impress them and bend in.

- Sexuality talks with preteens and teens who have difficulties with eye contact may work better if you are not sitting face to face. Try talking while you walk side by side, work alongside each other, or drive together in the car.

- How you choose to teach the different sexuality topics will depend on how much understanding your child has. Elucidate to your child, then back it up with visual and auditory input in the form of social stories. If required, do a task analysis or put up a word or picture schedule. All children on the spectrum can learn about human sexuality, even if it takes them longer to learn than their peers. It's finding out how to teach them that is the key.

Exercise

1. *What challenges have you encountered as a result of not observing relationship/sexual safety tips?*

_____

_____

_____

_____

2. *When the aforementioned challenges occurred, what would you have done differently?*

_____

_____

_____

_____

3. *What other safety practices have you employed over the months and years that have helped you immensely?*

_____

_____

_____

_____

f. Workplace Safety

Individuals with ASD are talented and esteemed employees in a lot of businesses and organizations. However, challenges with behaviors and social skills can make some workplace circumstances tough to traverse. Adults with ASD can be susceptible to bullying, isolation, and harassment in the workplace. It takes employer support and partnership to fashion positive, effective, and safe work environments. The most vital thing for parents to remember is that the business community is going to treat your loved one like everyone else; your loved one's supervisor is not going to have the same understanding as you. Hence, the goal should always be to establish and maintain clear hopes.

Telling others about your diagnosis can be a noteworthy first step. It is, nevertheless, a very personal decision. Some individuals find that full or partial disclosure can lead to more positive and productive work experiences.

Sharing this information also can back ASD awareness in the workplace, as well as proliferates occasions for communication on any needs for accommodations. Disclosure often starts with the employer's human resources department or with a direct supervisor. Parents can talk about this process with their loved one and ensure that the adult is ready for the initial and subsequent conversations. Also, it should be noted that disclosure is the foundation for certain workplace antiharassment protections, which may be critical down the road.

While adults with ASD would probably take workplace rules and regulations more seriously than their typical counterparts, the probability of things going wrong increases when the rules are either unwritten or nonexistent. If your loved one needs guidance concerning the social aspects of the workplace, then suggest that they find a mentor who can provide coaching or answer questions as desired.

There also are circumstances in which an individual with ASD might put themselves, their coworkers, or their employer in jeopardy because of curiosity or fascination. Even though employers will have some flexibility, when it comes to problems of safety and disregard for protocols, no second chances are guaranteed, regardless of how understanding a supervisor might be. In situations where rules have not been recognized, continuously inspire your loved one to ask for consent instead of for forgiveness. Much like disclosure, employer and staff education about ASD can be a powerful tool. While your loved one still needs to be their advocate at work, increased awareness ensures that colleagues will be more attuned to their needs.

Exercise

1. *What challenges have you encountered as a result of not observing workplace safety tips?*

_____

_____

_____

_____

2. *When the aforementioned challenges occurred, what would you have done differently?*

_____

_____

_____

_____

3. *What other workplace safety practices have you employed over the months and years that have helped you immensely?*

_____

_____

CHAPTER SEVEN

Life Skills—Self-determination/Advocacy

The general description of self-advocacy is to stand up for one's self by speaking up and asking for what one wants. Self-advocacy consists of knowing when and how to approach others to discuss anticipated goals, build improved mutual understanding and trust, and accomplish fulfillment and productivity. Effective self-advocacy regularly involves an amount of exposé about oneself to reach the goal of better shared understanding.

Ideally, parents lay the foundation for self-advocacy when the child is young. A central requirement for successful self-advocacy and disclosure is self-awareness. People with ASD need to realize how autism affects their dealings with others and the environment. Also, they need to be acquainted with their strengths and challenges. A parent or caretaker can do this with a child from a very early age; the earlier a child has an explanation about their differences, the better off they would be. Parents should educate their children about their strengths in any way they can. In addition to developing greater self-understanding, talents can be nurtured for future academic and professional pursuits.

a. Developing Self-Advocacy Skills

Everyone self-advocates, but it's a little different if the person has autism. Developing advocacy skills is a process that takes time; so learning to advocate for small things at an early age can build advocacy skills that will have lifelong profits. Individuals with severe ASD are unable to self-advocate due to major communication issues. However, they can easily overcome this barrier, as they can learn how to best communicate their needs and wants. A child throwing a tantrum is self-advocating, although not in the most effective way. In the case of an individual with ASD, regardless of verbal abilities, finding an effective method of communicating is critical.

Teaching self-advocacy can begin at a very young age. One way to build self-advocacy skills is by providing occasions to make choices. Give the child a choice between two or three things, and to make it easier on the child, pick one or two things that you know the child doesn't like and pair them with something highly desired. This will help develop decision-making skills that can be increasingly expanded.

Being comfortable with making decisions and speaking up about predilections and needs is crucial for developing independence as an adult. It is necessary for college-aged students and adults with ASD to advocate for their needs when communicating with instructors, friends, and colleagues. If they don't, there may be misunderstandings that may arise such that they may miss occasions to participate in class, social events, or in a work environment.

Also, a lot of people with ASD tend to express themselves better in writing than verbally. Therefore, coworkers and friends need to know that the individual with ASD needs more time to express themself verbally than they do in writing. This can help avoid any misconceptions. Developing advocacy skills takes time and effort. As the individual with ASD goes through the transitions of life, they'll need to self-advocate more and more. In the end, this will help them become more independent.

Exercise

1. *What has been your challenge when it comes to speaking up for yourself?*

_____

_____

_____

_____

2. *Has speaking up for yourself ever played out to your advantage? If yes, how?*

_____

_____

_____

_____

3. *What are the best ways that you prefer to effectively communicate?*

_____

_____

_____

_____

4. *What have been your frustrations when it comes to people being patient with you when you are trying to communicate?*

_____

_____

Most neurotypical individuals self-advocate for themselves through a blend of observation, practice, and self-reflection. But most individuals with ASD need direct instruction on self-advocacy because of their difficulties reading nonverbal cues. Real-life situations can be used to familiarize the individual with good self-advocacy practice with the help of an advocacy partner. By the end of the process, the advocacy partner merely serves as a resource to be tapped if and when needed.

b. The Benefits of Teaching Self-Advocacy Skills

Teaching how to self-advocate is essential, as one would not always be around to advocate for the young adult, and it's important to help them build the confidence they need to learn, work, and live comfortably. Teaching self-advocacy skills offers many crucial benefits:

- It shapes self-confidence.

- It lets them appreciate the power of positive thinking, making the most of their truth and using their gifts to achieve their goals.

- It promotes peace and acceptance, teaching society to embrace disability and improve living for all people with autism or other disabilities.

- It helps them achieve capricious levels of independence, as they learn to communicate their explicit needs and utilize their talents.

c. Tips for Teaching Self-Advocacy

Parents may have grown comfortable advocating for their child; however, this knowledge and skill must eventually be transferred to young adults, even though it may be difficult to define when they are ready. Below are tips for teaching the critical skill of self-advocacy:

i. Teach them about ASD. Individuals with ASD need to know what autism is to understand exactly how they are affected by it. Even though autism is a complex neurological condition, they can learn some of the rudimentary diagnostic criteria, and you can embolden them to read the writings of other self-advocates who describe autistic living. Autism affects individuals in different ways, but individuals who are affected should at least understand how they are precisely affected and how this plays out in their daily lives.

ii. Teach them how to articulate their strengths and weaknesses. It's the job of parents to nourish strengths and offer support to tackle weaknesses. But honest, personal appraisal of strengths and weaknesses is tough for both youngsters with autism and neurotypical youngsters alike. Begin by asking your child to try and ascertain their strengths and weaknesses. Then provide them with additional instances and how much they impact their life on a daily basis. Remember to emphasize that everyone has strengths and weaknesses and that the more self-aware one is, the greater opportunity they would have for growth.

iii. Practice <u>when</u> to disclose their needs. It's essential to help the child learn that self-advocacy is important, but there is a time and a place for full disclosure. Teach the child to ask for their needs, but not to overshare. Experts say teaching your child the difference between needs and preferences is crucial. Give instances where it might be suitable to demand a specific accommodation and when the individual can either delay or achieve a preference on their own.

iv. Practice <u>how</u> to disclose their condition. You can teach your child how to disclose their specific needs to avoid being vulnerable. They can be taught to disclose their needs and condition to teachers, disability advocates, or employers, depending on the child's actual situation. You can help them practice saying a statement that explains their most important needs. You could also help them type a statement specific to the educational needs that they could give to new teachers.

v. Teach them to find and utilize appropriate resources. A critical skill to self-advocacy is knowing how to recurrently find resources to meet one's needs. This implies finding the right people to articulate their needs too. Tell your child about specific advocacy and disability support organizations that have a wider appreciation of disability policy and resources on local, state, and national levels.

CHAPTER EIGHT

Life Skills—Consolidating Independence

a. Daily Walks and Practices

Change is sometimes dreadful; however, it is a necessity and must be embraced such that its appearance promotes rather than interrupts good living. For individuals with ASD, independent living may be tough at first, as they try to familiarize themselves with their new environment, doing things on their own and by themselves; but eventually, as they get a hang of a few things, formulate a routine that works for them, and get settled in, life becomes easier to traverse.

When times of distress come around, individuals with ASD must learn to go through them like every other person, even if they, unlike other people, would have peculiar experiences due to their unique conditions. In times of distress, adults with ASD can employ the following strategies, alongside other autism resources to focus on two main areas, namely *maintaining routines* and *prioritizing self-care.*

- Maintain connections with family, friends, supports, and others who are important to you. If you can't visit them as often as you might like, make use of the phone, social media, and other tools.

- Be cautious about mingling with others. It is possible that you may experience emotional blending with others, taking in emotions from them a bit too much, leading to you being overwhelmed and causing a shutdown.

- Nature can be very uplifting; so get outside on bright, sunny days. Whether you're walking or riding your bike, always put safety first; be properly clothed when heading out, use a helmet and maintain cordial relations with others.

- Maintain your routine as much as possible. Granted, when there is a situation that necessitates a slight change, such as bad weather, an emergency at work, or a citywide pandemic, it would be tough for your day to be business as usual. However, as much as it depends on you and your living space, you can stick to what still works on your daily routine and wait out the rest of the day for the distress to pass.

- When heading out, bring as little as possible, except for must-have items such as hand gloves, winter hats, masks, and so on. In addition, you can plan how much cash you'll bring in advance, or use credit cards.

- Set up a procedure for returning home and disinfecting items. This includes the following:

  o Leave shoes in the garage or by the door; label inside and outside shoes.

  o Wipe down surfaces.

  o Put worn clothes in the washer or a separate, isolated area before heading to the laundromat

- Have your emergency contacts handy. It is advised that you never go out without these contacts or without notifying them.

This is important, as they are the first contacts to be reached in case of any emergency. In addition, when heading out, turn on your mobile tracker, and send your location to your emergency contact so that they can find you if need be.

Exercise

1. *What has been your challenge with regard to independent living?*

_____

_____

_____

_____

2. *What steps have you taken to suitably manage to live independently?*

_____

_____

_____

_____

3. *What other tips have helped you immensely to cope with times of distress?*

_____

_____

_____

_____

4. *What emergency situations have you found yourself in, and how did you handle it?*

_____

_____

_____

_____

b. Exercise and Body Fitness

Experts say that young adults who participated in physical activity programs designed for individuals with ASD displayed significant gains in their social and communication skills. The activities comprised horseback riding, various types of group play, running/jogging programs, and excel-gaming, such as Nintendo Wii and other electronic games that involve physical activity. Furthermore, experts have added that when designed appropriately, physical activity programs can deliver a fun, safe scenery for networking with other young adults. In other words, they can offer exceptional occasions for practicing social skills. Additionally, activities involving animals such as horseback riding provide young people with a fun way to interact nonverbally as well as verbally.

It's particularly reassuring that expert analysis established that youth on the spectrum considerably improved their muscular strength and endurance by taking part in programs like exergaming, aquatic exercise, and horseback riding. This is principally important, as it is known from previous studies that people with ASD tend to have poorer muscular strength and endurance compared to neurotypical counterparts their age. Strength and endurance are essential for not only physical health but also for taking advantage of social openings that involve physical activity as well as recreational sports and nonstructured games.

A lot of individuals with ASD have lower fitness skills compared to other people. These skills comprise balance, body coordination, visual-motor control, and other mobility skills. Various types of physical activities improve skill-related fitness for youth with ASD. These activities comprise computer-based exergaming, jumping on a trampoline (with supervision and safety barriers), motor skill training such as table tennis, and horseback riding.

Exercise

1. *Do you participate in any form of exercise or body fitness?*

_____

_____

_____

_____

2. *What are your challenges as regards going to the gym?*

_____

_____

_____

_____

3. *How would you prefer the aforementioned limitations handled?*

_____

_____

_____

_____

4. If you do exercise, how has that affected your confidence and social skills?

_____

_____

_____

_____

c. Autism-Friendly Strategies for Encouraging Physical Activity

Research and our clinical experience have aided us in understanding and addressing a lot of autism-related hurdles that hinder the enjoyment of participation in physical activity. Numerous issues make the physical activity less attractive for a lot of people with ASD. These comprise poor social and motor skills, a penchant for screen-based activities, and lack of exercise partners and autism-friendly occasions for physical activity in our communities.

Here are some practical tips for encouraging regular physical activity:

i. Start small. As recommended by the CDC, children are required to get at least an hour of daily physical activity. While this is good to know, it can be hard to keep up with the numbers; so starting with a more modest goal and building from there is more ideal. Having shorter periods of physical activity, spaced all through the day, tend to be easier to sustain. Have it in mind that the goal is to make physical activity a steady and enjoyable part of daily life. So patient and long-term considerations are required.

Here are a few ways to add physical activity into a daily routine:

- Walking to school or work; if this cannot be done all the way, then at least some of the way.

- Walking the dog.

- Turn TV advertisements into exercise breaks—a few minutes of a rigorous activity such as jumping jacks.

- Make a regular family trip to the playground; if you can walk there, even better.

You can gradually increase the amount of time spent in these and other activities with the aim of eventually reaching the recommended daily hour of physical activity.

*ii. **Build motor skills.*** To successfully take part in physical activities and sports, have in mind that you would need to build some fundamental motor skills:

- Move-in different ways; run, jump, hop, and skip.

- Play with different sorts of equipment; like balls, bats, and racquets (e.g. throw, catch, kick and strike).

Practicing these skills at home can nurture your loved one's success in physical activities while increasing the likelihood that they would enjoy other socially engaging physical activities like playground games and recreational sports.

*iii. **Sample different sorts of physical activity.*** A wide range of activities is available for delivering the much-needed benefits. From table tennis to swimming, from riding bikes to riding horses, there's an abundance of physical activities that you or your loved one can try.

If possible, include one or more activities that encourage the following:

- Fitness: an activity that comprises moderate to vigorous exercise and gets a person breathing heavily.

- Social interaction: an activity that encompasses one or more other people, such as tennis or catch.

- Independence: an activity that can be done alone, like a home fitness or yoga routine, maybe with the help of a video.

iv. Bring in a role model and enlist friends and family. Parents are the most important role models for any child or young adult. If the adult with ASD is now independent and may not be close to their parents, an ideal role model can be employed to help them stay on course. Furthermore, friends and family can help on a daily or weekly basis, as they can lend helping hands any way they can. Also, ponder contacting the people who run recreational sports programs in your community. Some may fear that they lack the skills to absorb and include someone with ASD in their programs. Parents or caregivers may be able to give them the confidence they need by sharing strategies for communicating, motivating, and instructing.

CHAPTER NINE

Social Skills—Relationships

Even though young people with ASD occasionally appear to prefer to be by themselves, one of the most central issues, especially for older children and adults, is the development of friendships with peers. It can take some time and effort for people with ASD to develop the social skills required to interact efficaciously with others, and so it is imperative to begin developing social abilities early. What's more, bullying in middle and high school, not to mention at the workplace for some adults, can be a major concern for people with ASD, and the development of friendships is one of the best methods of prevention.

a. Personal Friendships

Generally, personal friendships are put together on one or more shared interests. Such kind of friends shares their thoughts and feelings as well as experiences. Some people on the autism spectrum have a habit of being very open, honest, and willing to share themselves with others; these are traits that close personal friends will value.

b. Close Personal Friends

Generally, close friends will stick up for each other in front of others, answer questions honestly and with kindness, help each other when there is a necessity, and enjoy spending time together. Most people, whether neurotypical or on the autism spectrum, only have a few friends who fit this description of a close personal friend.

c. Casual Acquaintances and Coworkers

Generally, casual acquaintances are platonic. They may not be as ready to be open, honest, and share personal information about themselves with others, and so they feel uncomfortable when another person shares too much about themself too soon. Some neurotypical adults like to develop friendships slowly. So when someone asks questions about one themselves, they are demonstrating that they have a conceivable interest in becoming friends. However, that doesn't imply that they will indeed become one's friend; it's only that they are interested in finding out whether they share enough interests to possibly become friends.

Making friends has less to do with whether people like a person than it does with whether the person has interests or experiences that are similar to theirs, and whether the person is also willing to share in the interests that are different from theirs. It's easy to lose potential friends if one shares more than they want to hear, or if one doesn't give them equal time to share their interests as well.

A lot of people with ASD have predominantly strong interests in certain areas. Unfortunately, it might be that very few other individuals share those interests. Clubs, where people with shared special interest are likely to meet, are excellent places to find and make friends. The Internet might also be a place where one can find people who share similar special interests. They might not live in close proximity to a person, but one can still exchange ideas and discuss their favorite topics virtually.

Exercise

1. What has been your biggest challenge when it comes to forming friendships?

_____

_____

_____

_____

2. What has been your experience with the following?

- *Close friends*

_____

_____

_____

_____

- *Personal friends*

_____

_____

_____

_____

- *Acquaintances*

_____

_____

_____

_____

3. What strategies have you used in the past that yielded the formation of new friendships?

_____

_____

d. Dating and Relationships

Almost everyone with ASD has a desire to go on a date sometime; however, it can be a huge struggle to go out on a date and be successful as there are a lot of things they struggle with. Nevertheless, one can successfully date an individual with ASD and have all the fun in the world. And for a person with ASD, the odds of getting a second date would be a lot better if the following tips are remembered:

i. Be yourself. Nothing is more essential than to be yourself. You will not impress your date by being someone you're not. Why the person chose to go out on a date with you is simply because, but isn't limited to the fact, that you are you, not someone else. The desire to be like another person or act a certain way to get the best from your date isn't going to work.

ii. Dress nicely. It is always recommended that you look nice when in public and this is a must when you're on a date. Wear clothes that make you look good; no need for hats, sweats, or ugly shirts of any kind. If it's winter period and cold, wear a nice coat. Inasmuch as people with ASD can be picky about how they dress, still, try to dress the best you can.

iii. Have good personal hygiene. Do take a shower and put on deodorant, cologne, or perfume. It is important that you smell good on a date. This will do wonders for your self-esteem and confidence, and it will keep your date from being uncomfortable around you. Plus, if you get a hug at the end of the date, you don't want to smell like garbage.

*iv. **Have good dental hygiene***. Brush your teeth, floss, and use mouthwash. Chew a mint or a piece of gum after eating too. This will help in keeping your breath fresh, ready for any close-up conversation. Keep this as well as possible, because you don't want your date to be turned off by your breath.

*v. **Have good table manners***. If you are at a table for dinner or any other meal, having good table manners is a necessity. This can be tough for someone with ASD, however, it can be worked on. Don't make bodily noises, eat too fast, or be messy in any way. If the meal placed before you doesn't appeal to you, kindly have it removed without making a scene.

*vi. **Be a gentleman or a lady***. You can be a gentleman in a number of ways, like offering to pick up the bill, holding the door open, opening the car door, and pulling the chair out for the lady. If you have a compliment, don't be scared to give it; just don't focus on physical appearances, as you can think of other things to compliment on too. Ladies like compliments more than you know.

For ladies, you can be ladylike by being courteous, smiling, talking respectfully, and being gentle with your many approaches.

*vii. **Ask your date questions***. It is important to show your date that you're interested in them. Ask them questions about themselves. However, do not ask too many questions, and be sensitive to know when to stop pressing for answers. Sometimes, questions can be too personal to be answered.

*viii. **Listen***. If you listen more during the date instead of doing all the talking, your date will definitely know you're interested, and they'll trust you more.

ix. Say goodnight properly. Once the date night comes to an end, and your date wants a handshake, give them a handshake. If they're comfortable with a hug, give them a hug. If they want a goodnight kiss, don't hesitate. Make sure you ask them to text or call you to let you know they got home safe, and you do the same.

x. Don't be needy on the follow-up. It can be very hard for someone with ASD to not dwell on how the date went. However, it is important not to appear needy. If the date went well, then the future is left to be seen; if it didn't, then you can prepare better next time. Let things happen naturally.

Dating is tough notwithstanding of disability, but with a disability it can be tougher. It's not unmanageable though if you follow some of these tips.

Exercise

1. *What are some of the challenges you faced when you went out on a date?*

_____

_____

_____

_____

2. *Which of the aforementioned tips helped you immensely while on a date?*

_____

_____

_____

_____

3. *What did you appreciate very well about your date and why?*

_____

_____

_____

_____

4. *What did your date appreciate about you and why?*

_____

_____

_____

_____

e. Love Fixations

A common characteristic of an individual with ASD is the predisposition to develop intense interests in specific topics or even in people. This intense attention can be helpful when it comes to being knowledgeable or having expertise in a topic, although it could be misunderstood by some who appear to be the focus of the fixation. Barring the best of intentions, intense attention can feel threatening to someone else. It is important to ensure reciprocation from the other party before making your next move.

f. Online Dating

A majority of people meet online these days, and dating sites can be a great forum for connecting with other people. Here are some essential things to keep in mind when it comes to online dating:

- Electronic communication can be hard to interpret since there is no tone of voice, facial expression, context, or other clue to help. This applies to both sending and receiving electronic messages. Take the time to make clear and ponder potential interpretations before sending.

- Remember that all information you put out on the Internet can hardly be erased. Be careful with what you send and share, and make sure you ask yourself if it is something you are comfortable with others seeing. You can run things by a friend for support and counsel before sending.

- Always trust your suspicions. If something doesn't feel right with someone you are communicating with, stop communicating with them, and if possible, block the person.

- Set up a video date before you decide to meet, so that you can get to know the person face to face and see if it's someone you may be interested in meeting in person.

- If you ultimately decide to meet in person, make sure that you follow the necessary safety precautions. Do not meet your date in a secluded place or at odd hours, at least not for the first time.

- Follow all of the other safety tips about relationship and sexuality too.

- Once you feel safe and ready, remember to have fun!

g. Rejection

Rejection is a part of life, howbeit it can be the worst, for everyone. It can hurt, feel surprising, and confusing. It's OK for you to say that you are not comfortable with something or someone; similarly, your potential date can say no, even if you thought they were equally interested in you. Regrettably, dating doesn't always follow concrete rules, and feelings can change. We seldom ever get clear reasons for these changes, but we have to accept that both people have to be on the same page about what they want.

h. Reading and Sending Signals

The social signals involved in dating and flirting can be multifaceted, unpredictable, and subtle. Understanding them presents a challenge for everyone. It can be most difficult when ASD obstructs the ability to read and respond to social signals. This can yield confusion, discomfort, and frustration. When social cues are missed, your potential date may feel that their messages or feelings aren't being heard or reciprocated. It usually would take some extra attention and communication on your part, even if it means asking follow-up questions and clarifying if you are not sure about how to interpret a subtle cue.

CHAPTER TEN

Social Skills—Societal Connections

a. Housing

Whether an adult with ASD carries on living at home or moves into the community is determined largely by their ability to manage everyday tasks with little or no supervision. A lot of families prefer to begin with a supported living arrangement and then move toward greater independence.

b. Supervised Group Home

A supervised group home typically serves more than a few people with disabilities. These homes are characteristically located in middling family houses in residential neighborhoods. Trained professionals are employed to aid each resident based on individual needs. The residents usually have jobs away from home during the day.

c. Supervised Apartment

A supervised apartment might be appropriate for those who desire to live with fewer people but still need some supervision and assistance. There is typically no daily supervision in this situation, however someone comes by several times a week. The residents are responsible for getting to work, preparing meals, and meeting personal care and housekeeping needs. A supervised apartment is a good step in transitioning to independent living.

d. Independent Living

In independent living, individuals live in their apartments or houses and necessitate little, if any, support services from outside agencies. Services might be present but restricted to helping with compound problem-solving issues rather than day-to-day living skills. For example, some people might require help managing money or handling government bureaucracy. It is also essential for those living independently to have a *buddy* who lives nearby and can be contacted for support. Coworkers, friends, local business employees, or other community members could be unified into a support system, whether informally through social interaction or as part of a more organized effort.

Adulthood for people with ASD isn't all about getting a job and living in a particular area; it also has to do with making friends and having a sense of belonging in a community. People with ASD may need assistance in encouraging friendships and structuring time for special interests. A lot of the support systems developed in the early years may be of continued use, as they can provide dependability and a framework for expansion.

e. Employment

Generally, employment takes advantage of an individual's strengths and abilities. Jobs should typically have a well-defined goal or endpoint, and bosses must recognize one's social limitations. It is recommended that parents begin helping their loved ones find jobs before they leave grade school, to prepare them with job skills and experience. There are three types of employment possibilities:

i. Competitive employment. This is the most independent form of employment. It requires little or no support offered in the work environment. Some people might be thriving in vocations that require focus on details, but then again require only limited social interaction with colleagues, like computer sciences, research or library sciences. It could also help to ask for accommodations, such as a workspace without glowing lights to feel more comfortable at work.

ii. Self-employment. Self-employment is also an option some people with ASD seek to pursue. This, however, requires strong motivation and determination but can be more flexible than working for a company or the government.

iii. Supported employment. Support employment is a system that lets people with ASD pursue paid employment in the community, on occasion, as part of a mobile crew, and at other times, individually in a job developed for them.

iv. Secure or sheltered employment. Secure or sheltered employment guarantees an individual with ASD a job in a facility-based setting. People in secure settings generally receive work skills and behavior training as well, while sheltered employment might not provide training that would allow for more independence.

Once you are ready to look for employment, start by contacting agencies that may be of help, like the state employment offices, vocational rehabilitation departments, social service offices, mental health departments, and disability-specific organizations. A lot of these agencies, as well as other valuable services and supports, can be found in the Autism Society's nationwide online database.

f. Workplace Skills

Here are a few workplace skills to develop:

i. Communication skills. Good communication skills are critical for helping you to work successfully, form solid relationships, and avert needless misunderstandings. In a workplace, it is well-mannered to engage in *small talk*. Small talk is a short, casual conversation typically about fairly impersonal, everyday topics, such as the weather, hobbies and interests, weekend plans or holiday plans, and news headlines or current affairs. Small talk may seem to be commonplace or without purpose, but it plays a very important part in social interaction.

Here are some of the reasons why it is imperative to try to use small talk:

- It is a great way to start a conversation.

- It helps to maintain social relationships.

- It shows that you are being friendly.

- It is a polite and safe way of talking to someone you don't know very well.

- It can lead to other conversations.

- It is a good way of ensuring that you are not going to be too personal or offend anyone in conversation.

Examples of topics of conversations in the workplace

- The weather
- Work
- Transport
- TV
- Films
- Hobbies (when appropriate)
- Holidays
- Sports

Topics to avoid:

- Religion

- Politics
- Disability
- Personal relationships
- Salary
- Review meetings/work meetings
- Cultural judgments
- Talk behind someone's back/gossip
- Negative comments about the workplace
- Tell other people you can do their job better than them

ii. Social skills. In a lot of ways, being friendly with the people you work with is very parallel to being friendly with friends and family. Nevertheless in other ways, it's very different. It is recommended that you learn some of the social etiquettes of the workplace so that you can fit in and feel comfortable with your coworkers.

One of the foremost challenges of individuals living with ASD is understanding social rules. Social rules are the rules that apply to countless social situations. You have perhaps found them quite tough, especially as the rules often change the subject on where you are and who you are with. The workplace has its own set of social rules that you need to know. If someone is supporting you in the workplace, helping you understand the social rules of your particular work can be part of how they help you.

iii. Organization skills. When confronted with a lot of different demands on your time at work, it is imperative to organize and order the workload and effectively manage time. When trying to implement an organized approach to work tasks, consider the following points:

1. Be aware of all your work tasks. Make a list of all your main activities to help you get a summary of the time you will need to set aside. This should make it easier for you to arrange tasks.

2. Be realistic about what is involved and how long will it take. Break down your work tasks, and be truthful as to the time you will need to set aside to complete them.

3. Prioritize. To effectively prioritize our time, consider the following questions:

- What is urgent?

- What is routine?

- What can be prepared for?

- What are the consequences?

4. Map it out. Determine what needs to be done, when to do it, and how to do it. Once you have developed a clear idea of what your work tasks are, you can begin to make plans. A timetable or action plan can be a useful resource to help you stay organized at work.

5. Establish routine and structure. Establishing structure to your daily work will help set the defined tasks for the day or week ahead. Structure can be established by doing the following:

- setting a timetable or calendar for each day or week

- writing a to-do list or checklist of tasks

- setting reminders or alarms to keep you on track

- setting daily or weekly goals (as identified by your manager)

6. Evaluate progress. Ask yourself or your manager how to get on, whether you're on schedule, and what can be done to get back on schedule. It is essential that you take time to evaluate how efficiently you

are completing work tasks. You may need to reassess timetables and action plans if work tasks are not being completed to schedule.

iv. Time management skills. Some tips for managing time:

- After prioritizing your tasks, make a to-do list, and work through it in priority order.

- Clear your desk, and plan your activities for the next day.

- List your time-specific tasks, for example team meetings.

- Ensure that you have set aside enough time to plan your day/week.

- Do difficult jobs first thing in the morning when you are at your best.

- Complete minor tasks when you have less energy at the end of the day.

- Try to arrange set times for tasks so that you can keep track of your progress.

- When you start a piece of work, try to finish it.

- Assess how you use your time; are you making effective use of it?

- Work towards deadlines; if you are behind schedule, reassess, ask for help, or agree to new deadlines.

g. Dealing with Difficult People and Bullying

Unfortunately, meeting and having to deal with difficult people and bullies can occur in the workplace; for some persons with ASD, it is a nightmare that they experienced in school and that they wish never to experience again. There are various levels of possibilities that you would encounter a difficult superior or a coworker who enjoys getting on your nerves.

h. Responding to Reports of Workplace Bullying

For managers of the office workspace, successfully responding to issues when they occur can arrest the situation both now and in the future. Prompt actions can also buttress to workers that workplace bullying is frowned upon and consistently by the organization. The table below sets out the principles that should be applied when handling reports of workplace bullying.

Response	Measure
Act on time	Respond to reports quickly, reasonably, and within established timelines. Appropriate parties should be advised of how long it will likely take to respond to the report and should be kept informed of the progress.
Treat all reports seriously	All reports should be taken seriously and evaluated on their merits and facts.
Maintain discretion	The confidentiality of all parties involved should be preserved. Details of the matter should only be known by those directly involved in the complaint or in resolving it.
Ensure bureaucratic fairness	The person who is alleged to have committed the bullying behavior should be treated as innocent unless the reports are proven to be true. Reports must be put to the person they are made against, and that person must be given an occasion to explain themself. The person reporting the bullying should be heard and their report treated as credible and reliable unless proven otherwise. The chance to have decisions reviewed should be clarified to all parties.

Be neutral	Impartiality toward everyone involved is critical, including the way people are treated throughout the process. The person responding to the report should not have been directly involved, and they should also avoid personal or professional bias.
Support all parties	Once a report has been made, the parties involved should be told what support is available, for instance, employee assistance programs, and allowed a support person to be present at interviews or meetings such as a health and safety representative, union representative, or work colleague.
Do not victimize	It is imperative to ensure that anyone who reports workplace bullying is not victimized for doing so. The person accused of workplace bullying and witnesses should also be protected from victimization.
Communicate process and outcomes	All parties should be informed of the process, how long it will take, and what they can expect will happen during and at the end of the process. Should the process be delayed for any reason, all parties should be made aware of the delay and advised when the process is expected to resume. Finally, reasons for actions that have been taken and in some circumstances not taken should be explained to the parties.
Keep records	The following should be recorded:

- the person who made the report
- when the report was made
- who the report was made to
- the details of the issue reported
- action taken to respond to the issue, and
- any further action required – what, when, and by whom.

Records should also be made of conversations, meetings, and interviews detailing who was present and the agreed outcomes.

i. Hygiene

It's essential to look professional and smell good at work. Good personal hygiene is central, as it helps in the prevention of the transfer of illnesses and maintenance of appearance.

Begin by maintaining a fresh breath. Clean teeth are simple to arrange; just brush twice daily, and floss once a day. If sensory problems are standing in your way, you can always get help. Also, a regular visit to the dentist will do your mouth a world of good. Beware of body odor.

Wearing fresh undies every day, and changing clothes often are equally important. Nobody likes to smell body odor, and neither do you. Shower regularly, a couple of times a day if need be. Wear deodorant unless you just can't bear it. If fear of changing clothes or dislike of laundry powder smells is holding you back, ask a trusted friend for help.

j. Managing Stress and Anxiety at Work

Everyone can get tensed at work, and feeling stressed at times is quite normal. What is most important is knowing how to handle your stress. Here are some useful strategies to handle stress:

- Identify what triggers stress and try to calm down before things worsen.

- Get enough sleep.

- Eat healthy foods, as low blood sugar can contribute to feeling irritable.

- Learn to relax; Yoga or meditation can help.

- Plan activities each day that you will look forward to.

- Do some exercise, as this helps with relaxation.

- Set realistic goals, and stick to a routine.

- Plan and organize work tasks, without overcommitting.

- Try to have a positive attitude.

- Don't worry about the little things.

- Talk to family and friends outside the workplace.

k. Health-Care Transition

According to a new study by the CDC, adolescents with ASD are the least likely among young people with mental, behavioral, and developmental conditions to receive guidance from their doctor on the shift from pediatric to adult health care. Only about 9 percent of adolescents with ASD received transition planning compared with about 20 percent of those with emotional disorders and 15 percent of those with behavioral disorders.

This nationwide descriptive study is the first to focus on transition health-care planning for children with specific mental, behavioral, and developmental disorders (MBDDs), according to experts at the CDC National Center on Birth Defects and Developmental Disabilities.

In addition, the analysis found that about 16 percent of adolescents with MBDDs and about 14 percent without received the recommended transition-planning guidance.

l. Filling the Gap

Here a few tips to help you prepare for this new phase of life.

- Have a conversation with your family and current pediatrician about the next steps.

- Stay organized.

- Determine how you will organize your information (e.g., digitally: phone, or consider purchasing a binder/notebook.

- Find a doctor who best fits your needs and understands you as an individual.

m. Driving

Driving is a big step for teens and young adults on the autism spectrum. It's one of many choices individuals with ASD make as a part of the transition to adulthood. Driving can contribute to the development of the individual, improving access to community activities, employment opportunities, and social relationships.

n. Driving Readiness

It is important to answer a few questions before you or your young adult consider if it's time to begin driving. These questions should border around mental health and maturity, age requirement, governing laws, mental and bodily disciplines, and so on. In addition, a trip to the doctor for a thorough medical exam will be a great idea before commencing.

o. Safety First

It must be stated that there are laws against driving with ASD, but safety is important. Driving can be stressful and challenging in a lot of ways; people with ASD may struggle more to adapt to the rapid change and thus need to be thoroughly guided all the way.

Consider some of the important factors and skills that are involved with driving:

- social judgment

- motor coordination

- preplanning

- flexibility to change

- ability to focus

- multitask

- prioritize

Get the Letter of Intent for Free

Building a relationship with our readers is the very best thing about writing. We occasionally send newsletters with details on new releases, special offers, and other bits of news relating to autism and special needs.

And if you sign up to the mailing list, we'll send you the Letter of Intent E-book, which is worth $35.00, for free. You can get Letter of Intent, for free, by signing up at http://eepurl.com/M2105.

About the Letter of Intent E-book:

No one else knows your child as well as you do, and no one ever could. You are a walking encyclopedia of your child's history, experiences, habits, and wishes. If your child has special needs, the family's history adds a helpful chapter to your child's book, one detailing his unique medical, behavioral, and educational requirements.

A letter of intent helps your loved ones and your child manage a difficult transition when you no longer are the primary caregiver. A letter of intent is an important planning tool for parents of children with special needs (including adult children), and also guides your child's future caregivers in making the most appropriate life decisions for your child, including providing direction to your child's trustee in fulfilling his or her fiduciary responsibilities.

The letter of intent may be addressed to anyone you wish.

This document addresses the following points:

- emotional information,

- future vision for the child,

- biographical and personal information,

- medical information,

- personality traits and preferences,

- habits and hygiene,

- meals and dietary requirements, and

- much more.

Once you prepare, sign, and date the letter of intent, you should review the document annually and update it as necessary. It is important that you let your child's potential future caregiver know that the letter of intent exists and where it can be accessed; even better, you can review the document with the caregiver on an annual basis. The letter of intent should be placed with all of your other relevant legal and personal documents concerning your child.

Found This Book Useful? You Can Make a Big Difference

Reviews are the most powerful tools in our arsenal when it comes to getting attention for our books. Much as we'd like to, we don't have the financial muscle of a New York publisher. We can't take out full page ads in the newspaper or put posters on the subway.

But we do have something much more powerful and effective than that, and it's something that those publishers would kill to get their hands on.

A committed and loyal bunch of readers like you.

Honest reviews of our books help bring them to the attention of other readers.

If you've found this book useful, we would be very grateful if you could spend just five minutes leaving a review (it can be as short as you like) on the book's Amazon page. You can jump right to the page by clicking below.

Click here to leave reviews.

Thank you very much.

Other Books by Susan Jules

Have you read them all?

What will happen to my Special Needs Child when I am gone: A Detailed Guide to Secure Your Child's Emotional and Financial Future—https://geni.us/At0afS

Let's Talk: A Conversational Skills Workbook for Children with Autism & Special Needs— https://geni.us/dnl1

105 Activities for Your Child with Autism and Special Needs: Enable them to Thrive, Interact, Develop and Play—https://geni.us/tSu9

Life Skills Workbook for Children with Autism and Special Needs—https://www.amazon.com/Skills-Workbook-Children-Autism-Special/dp/B09232WH45

Life Skills Workbook for Teens with Autism and Special Needs—https://www.amazon.com/Skills-Workbook-Teens-Autism-Special/dp/B092CG3K7D/

Printed in Great Britain
by Amazon